CAREER TREK

Troy R. Nielson
Utah Valley State College

PEARSON
Prentice
Hall

Upper Saddle River, New Jersey
Columbus, Ohio

Library of Congress Cataloging-in-Publication Data

Nielson, Troy R.
  Career trek / Troy R. Nielson.
    p. cm.
  Includes bibliographical references and index.
  ISBN 978-0-13-119304-8 (pbk.)
  1. Vocational guidance. 2. Career development. 3. Self-evaluation.
  4. College graduates—Employment. I. Title.
HF5381.N54 2008
650.1—dc22   2007003547

Vice President and Executive Publisher: Jeffery W. Johnston
Executive Editor: Sande Johnson
Editorial Assistant: Lynda Cramer
Production Editor: Alexandrina Benedicto Wolf
Production Coordination and Text Design: Thistle Hill Publishing Services, LLC
Design Coordinator: Diane C. Lorenzo
Cover Designer: Jason Moore
Cover Image: Jupiter Images
Production Manager: Susan Hannahs
Director of Marketing: David Gesell
Marketing Manager: Amy Judd
Marketing Coordinator: Brian Mounts

This book was set in ITC Caslon by Integra Software Services. It was printed and bound by
R.R. Donnelley & Sons Company. The cover was printed by Phoenix Color Corp.

Pearson Education Ltd.
Pearson Education Singapore Pte. Ltd.
Pearson Education Canada, Ltd.
Pearson Education—Japan

Pearson Education Australia Pty. Limited
Pearson Education North Asia Ltd.
Pearson Educación de Mexico, S.A. de C.V.
Pearson Education Malaysia Pte. Ltd.

10 9 8 7 6 5 4 3 2 1
ISBN-13: 978-0-13-119304-8
ISBN-10:   0-13-119304-X

To my wife, Jennifer, whose wise advice, consistent support, and unconditional love have been essential to my career success

To my five children—Jocelyn, Christopher, Aubrey, Spencer, and Emily—who make all my career management efforts worthwhile

BRIEF CONTENTS

CONTENTS

TREK TASKS SUMMARY

PREFACE

When I joined the faculty of the College of Business Administration at California State University–San Marcos (CSUSM) in 1998, I was asked to develop a new elective course for undergraduate business students. No constraints on the type of course were imposed—one of the benefits from being a faculty member at a relatively young institution. My thoughts returned to my own undergraduate program, which I had completed only 7 years earlier. What course did I wish would have been part of that program? I desired a course with considerable practical value for the students that provided both short-term enjoyment and long-term impact. My thoughts led to a course on career development—but not devoted to the theoretical underpinnings of career choices—which provides practical tools and offers hands-on activities to enhance career success, regardless of the students' undergraduate major.

THE NEED FOR A CAREER DEVELOPMENT COURSE

Why the emphasis on career development? Isn't that something the career or placement services center already offers? Placement services usually only handle a subset of career-related activities, focusing primarily on helping graduating students land their first job. Students often know very little about the career placement services at their institutions and, therefore, don't avail themselves of these services.

My experience suggests that most seniors haven't given much thought about what they want to do after graduation, nor have they learned the fundamental principles of managing their careers effectively. Other students know what they want to do but are less certain about how to get there. This is due in part to the lack of attention given to career development in most university curricula. Most students focus so much on getting the degree that they pay minimal attention to what they will do with the degree.

Rich Sulpizio, former president and COO of Qualcomm, a San Diego–based telecommunications company, came and spoke to business students at CSUSM a few years ago. As he described his unfolding career, he exclaimed that if he were teaching a class on career development he would call it "The Tumbleweed Theory of Career Development." He explained that he never really engaged in career planning or purposefully mapped his career progression in advance. He worked very hard, performed well, received some good fortune, and was recruited to move from one job to another until he landed at Qualcomm. There are certainly other successful professionals who would subscribe to his approach.

There have been some unexpected changes in my own career—just like that tumbleweed suddenly blown by a shifting wind. If you had told me in 1991 as I completed my bachelor's degree that I would eventually earn a PhD and become a business professor, I would have replied, "Sure, and I will also replace Michael Jordan as the best basketball player on the planet." Okay, given my diminutive height and unexceptional leaping ability, the odds of my going into academia were much, *much* better than a hall-of-fame basketball career. Recently I had the opportunity to return to my undergraduate alma mater, Brigham Young University, as a visiting professor. This opportunity came at roughly the same time that I was promoted to associate professor and granted tenure at CSUSM, which is usually not the time when professors leave their existing institutions. My first point is that for all of our meticulous planning, our careers rarely unfold exactly as planned. Conversely, we rarely enjoy the career success Rich Sulpizio has experienced by being blown to and fro by the winds of changing occupational trends.

Students rarely give adequate thought to the time and money they invest in their degrees. They completely fail to recognize that the return on their investment is mainly dependent on how well they understand and use career management principles.

Investing in Your Education

As you start reading this book, think about the following question: How much money have I invested in earning a bachelor's degree? Let's assume that you finish your degree in the customary 4 years (yes, I know that some of you prefer the 6-year route). The average undergraduate student at a public university will spend about $125,000, calculated as follows:

Tuition & fees ($2,500 per semester × 8 semesters)	$20,000[1]
Parking ($125 per semester × 8 semesters)	$1,000
Books ($500 per semester × 8 semesters)	$4,000
Opportunity costs (job earning $25,000 per year × 4 years)	$100,000

For the purposes of this simple illustration, let's exclude the monetary costs of the time you spent on homework and other academic activities, transportation, housing, and food (because you would be spending that money anyway). So you are investing somewhere in the neighborhood of $125,000 to obtain your degree.

What were your reasons for obtaining the degree in the first place? It wasn't to strengthen your physical conditioning, although walking back and forth across campuses and carrying increasingly hefty textbooks may be accomplishing that purpose. Was it the social scene, the never-ending parties, or hanging out with friends? How about testing your patience as you wait in long lines or try to find a decent parking space? The more likely reasons were

- Increasing your future earning potential and chances for career success
- Enjoying the satisfaction of personal accomplishment and learning
- Fulfilling social pressures from family and friends to earn a college degree

---

[1] www.collegeboard.com. "2006–2007 College Costs." Average annual tuition and fees for a four-year public university are $5,836.

Investing in Your Career

Whatever your primary purpose for seeking a degree, the reality is that you have spent significant money and countless hours toward a career. *Thought-provoking question:* How much time, energy, and money have you spent on preparing for your career after graduation? If you are like I was as a student, and like 90% of the students who have taken my careers class, you have invested minimally in that effort. I'm going to let you in on a little secret. Earning a bachelor's, master's, or doctoral degree guarantees you *nothing*! Does that mean you have been wasting your time? Absolutely not! *Fortune* magazine career columnist Anne Fisher makes the following observations:

> That college degree really is (surprise!) every bit as valuable as your parents kept telling you it would be. Three-quarters of Americans aged eighteen to thirty-four don't have one, and that is significant. . . . You yourself, as an energetic, bright college grad, are a scarce resource right now.[2]

The point I am trying to make is that your degree, while an important step, is only an admission ticket to the dance. You still need to pick the right dance partner, keep learning new dance steps, and package yourself in such a way that somebody will want to dance with you. Almost all professional jobs today require that you have a college degree just to be considered for the position. A college degree is neither a necessary nor a sufficient variable when predicting career success. It is not a necessary variable because individuals can be successful without a college degree (ask Bill Gates or Michael Dell). However, the odds of that happening are not good, and a college degree increases your business opportunities and improves your money-making potential. The degree is not a sufficient variable because there are many college graduates whose careers flounder. You obviously need more than a piece of paper and a credential to have a successful career, even when that paper represents the blood, sweat, and tears of many years.

Most students focus so heavily on completing the degree that they forget why they wanted it in the first place. Over the years, when I have asked students at the beginning of the careers course to indicate where they were in their career decision process, typically 60 to 70% had no idea what they wanted to do after graduation—and most of them were seniors. The question "What do I want to be when I grow up?" is still prevalent among many seasoned professionals. The effective placement services offered at most universities assist students with résumés and setting up interviews with companies that come to campus, but they don't usually help students learn how to manage and develop their careers. *Learning key principles and tools to improve your odds of an effective career is the purpose of this book.*

---

[2] Fisher, A. (2001). *If my career's on the fast track, where do I get a road map?* New York: HarperCollins, pp. 2–3.

THE NEED FOR A DIFFERENT CAREER DEVELOPMENT BOOK

I used multiple textbooks in my careers course with varying success and mixed reviews from my students. Additionally, I have perused several other career development books from major textbook publishing companies and found three problems:

1. They largely ignored the critical issue of fit (how well the person's motives and skills fit the demands and incentives of a specific job or career path).

2. They were written primarily for freshmen and sophomores rather than upper-division students (therefore, they lacked depth and seemed too basic for my business students).

3. They were written with a focus on general life skills (time management, budgeting, choosing a major, etc.) instead of career management skills.

Few of the textbooks suffered from all three deficiencies, and they each had redeeming qualities (e.g., excellent résumé examples, thorough chapters on interviewing skills). However, I could never find one that fully satisfied me or my students. Many of my students urged me to write my own book. I finally decided to take that leap of faith and launched into this endeavor, which has been a journey of its own.

The Theme

Several years ago I read Jon Krakauer's book *Into Thin Air,* which was about his disastrous attempts to climb Mount Everest in the late spring of 1996. As I thought about an analogy for the professional career journey in the 21st century, this book kept coming to mind. Just like Everest, professional careers are enticing to many but can also be intimidating when one is at the foot of the mountain looking up. Reaching the summit of Everest is the real appeal according to veteran climbers. I can only imagine what the view must look like at 29,028 feet above sea level. I'm not a mountain climber and I don't envision myself ever climbing Everest, but I know that world-class professionals in numerous occupations feel a similar exhilaration when they reach their career summits. Other similarities abound in this comparison between Mount Everest and "Mount Career."

Unexpected weather conditions and questionable decisions associated with the 1996 expeditions led to the deaths of 12 climbers, including many who had previously reached Everest's summit. Similarly, Mount Career leaves many professionals stranded on its slopes, stuck in jobs they don't want, and feeling too trapped to shift career direction.[3] Many of these careers have reached a plateau because of poor career decisions or inattention to career management. Other times, individuals' careers are casualties through no fault of their own, but as the

---

[3] My intention with this analogy is not to disrespect those who lost their lives on Everest, or their families and friends; I do not equate the loss of life with the loss of career.

result of organizational downsizing and reorganizations associated with mergers and acquisitions. Noted career scholar Douglas T. Hall made the following observation: "The career as we once knew it—as a series of upward moves, with steadily increasing income, power, status, and security—has died."[4]

He wrote the obituary on the "Organization Man" career in 1996. Long gone are the days of staying 30 years with the same organization and expecting the organization to ensure your career advancement. Navigating the terrain of today's careers can be treacherous indeed, resembling more of a lattice (involving frequent lateral moves) than the traditional career ladder (vertical moves).

Organization of This Book

Drawing from Krakauer's Everest account, I have incorporated many other useful characteristics of a high-mountain adventure into the organization of this book. The book has four sections, as follows.

Trek Overview. This section introduces fundamental principles of career success, such as person-job fit (Chapter 1) and managing your career as if you were a brand (Chapter 2). These chapters also emphasize the importance of passion and attitude to career success. Chapter 2 is a primer on major theories of career development discussed over the past 50 years and provides you with a high-level look at your unfolding career.

Base Camp. For 6 weeks prior to assaulting the face of Everest and attempting to reach the summit, Krakauer and other climbers resided 17,600 feet above sea level at base camp.[5] This camp has several purposes, the most important of which is the acclimatization of the climbers' bodies to the higher altitudes and thinner air. Other benefits include preparing and checking vital equipment, mapping out the ascent routes up the face of the mountain, becoming better acquainted with all members of the climbing expedition, and practicing specific mountaineering skills needed to reach the summit.

Our Career Trek Base Camp exists for similar reasons. Chapters 3 and 4 help you to identify your best skills, weaknesses, career aspirations, interests, and personality dimensions. Through self-assessment exercises you will uncover possible career paths that provide better potential fit given who you are and what you enjoy doing the most. Even if you have a well-defined career path, these assessments should bring new insights about yourself. *And knowing yourself is the first principle of effectively managing your career.* Chapter 5 will help you prepare and refine your vital equipment (professional résumé and cover letter. You will realize the importance of networking and working with others on your career trek (Chapter 6). Finally, Chapters 7 and 8 discuss several routes up the mountain and offer suggestions for researching these routes.

---

[4] Hall, D. T. (1996). *The career is dead—long live the career.* San Francisco: Jossey-Bass, p. 1.
[5] Krakauer, J. (1997). *Into thin air.* New York: Macmillan, chapter 6.

Ascending the Mountain. The most strenuous and frustrating activities take place in this portion of the trek. This section of the trek is dominated by the job search and hiring processes, particularly job interviewing activities. Chapter 9 discusses effective job search strategies to help you obtain more (and better) job leads. The next three chapters focus on interview preparation (Chapter 10), conducting a winning job interview (Chapter 11), and following up on the interview in a professional manner, along with providing strategies for negotiating and evaluating job offers (Chapter 12).

Reaching the Summit. You will not reach your career summit while reading this book—at least it is highly unlikely. However, Chapter 13 explains some important rules for career success, including crucial steps during your first year in a new position. For those who are considering changing jobs or career paths, Chapter 14 provides some ideas on making tough career decisions and dealing with work–life balance issues. Chapter 15 emphasizes long-term development through mentoring and talent renewal.

Book Features

Trek Tasks. Each chapter offers suggested activities, called Trek Tasks, that will help you apply the concepts to your own career circumstances. Your instructor may or may not require you to do these activities, but I would encourage you to do many of them on your own—it is *your* career after all.

Trek Lists. A summary in checklist format at the end of each chapter helps you remember the most important principles.

Expert Opinions. I have tried to integrate several perspectives and strategies from other successful professionals, including leaders of for-profit and not-for-profit organizations. One individual who has informed many of the principles in this book is David Bennett, an exemplary executive with Marriott, Mailboxes Etc., and Amen Clinics. He joined the CSUSM faculty several years ago to teach and help the business school develop external relationships. He and I developed one of the CSUSM business school's most innovative and popular courses, "In the Executive's Chair." Later, he also participated in many aspects of my career development course, lending both his experience and his professional network to enhance the learning potential for my students. Insights from David and other successful people are found throughout the text.

ALL CAREER CLIMBERS WELCOME

While my experience sharing these concepts has been primarily with business students, I have written this book for students at all levels and in all majors. The principles contained in *Career Trek* can be readily applied to different stages of your career and used independently. This book is intended as a primary text in career-related courses and as a supplemental text in more generalized life skills courses. It can also be applied in nonacademic settings by professionals who feel stuck or plateaued in their careers, who feel less than ecstatic about their current career direction, or who have recently graduated and are in the initial stages of their career journey.

When you finish *Career Trek* you should be well-prepared and enthusiastic to climb the career mountains that lie ahead (yes, you will likely climb more than one). I won't promise that you will feel the same level of awe and exhilaration as those who reach the summit of Everest, but you will feel a great sense of accomplishment as you use the career principles and activities to forge your own meaningful path up the mountain. You should also feel a stronger peace of mind in a career direction you have chosen because you have paid the price and done your homework.

So buckle up, grab your pack, and get ready for some thin air and tough breathing. This process is not a cakewalk and, as with most new opportunities, what you get out of this trek will mirror the effort you put into the journey. Don't let anxiety or fear overpower you. I will do everything in my power to guide you successfully to the completion of this trek. Let's go!

ACKNOWLEDGMENTS

This book would not exist if it weren't for the gentle prodding of my former students at CSUSM. I started writing this book at their request, and with them in mind as my primary audience. It was a privilege working with them and helping them, in some small way, embark on successful careers. I acknowledge the additional support from my students at Brigham Young University's Marriott School of Management and my current institution, Utah Valley State College (soon to be Utah Valley University). Specifically, I want to thank Adam Hopson for his months of researching material, suggesting modifications to PowerPoint slides, and editing earlier drafts of the chapters. His attention to detail and constructive feedback were beneficial.

Many colleagues have made vital contributions to this book. First and foremost is my good friend and mentor, David Bennett. David offered his professional insights on career-related issues from the perspective of a seasoned executive. He has also provided consistent encouragement and friendship to finish this labor of love to our students. He now teaches the careers class that I created. The students love him. I enjoyed my faculty colleagues in the College of Business Administration at CSUSM and express my appreciation particularly to Raj Pillai, Ben Cherry, Kathleen Watson, Glen Brodowsky, Regina Eisenbach, Dennis Guseman, and Keith Butler for their insights and encouragement related to this book. I also thank Pam Wells, Diana Sanchez, and Sandy Punch at the Career Center for their helpful insights and considerable hours spent with my students.

Colleagues at Brigham Young University (BYU) and Utah Valley State College (UVSC) have been equally supportive and encouraged the completion of the project. At BYU, I am grateful for Brooke Derr's passion for career development and for his permission to use the Career Success Map Questionnaire. At UVSC, I am grateful to Doug Miller for his personal support to both the book and my career success. I also appreciate Karen Whelan-Berry and Chuck Cozzens for being great team members and for their shared passion for our students' career success.

Many nonacademic colleagues contributed insights to this book, especially related to networking strategies. Two individuals whose time and ideas have been particularly beneficial are Pepper de Callier and Bob Uda. I thank them for sharing the wisdom learned from years of experience helping people with their careers and from their writings about career success factors. I also express appreciation to Scott Adams, creator of *Dilbert,* who provides me and so many other readers with a daily dose of workplace humor. The writings of many other authors, particularly those who have written career-related books and articles, have been most informative, and I acknowledge their influence on my own thoughts about career development.

I am grateful to the following reviewers for their constructive and thorough insights of earlier drafts: James M. Benshoff, University of North Carolina at Greensboro; Marilyn Joseph, Florida Metropolitan University; Patricia Locks, Howard Payne University; Mel Schnake, Valdosta State University; and Edison Wells, College of DuPage.

Furthermore, I acknowledge the important role played by my editor Sande Johnson, her assistant Lynda Cramer, and Alex Wolf at Pearson/Prentice Hall. Their timely guidance and consistent support were invaluable. I am grateful to Angela Urquhart and Amanda Dugan at Thistle Hill Publishing Services who made the production of this book a relatively painless process.

Finally, I thank my parents, Richard and Kathryn Nielson, for providing a loving home and for encouraging my career pursuits throughout my life. I appreciate my sisters, Brandi and Kelly, and my brother-in-law, Jason, for their personal support and much laughter along this journey. Most importantly, I express my love to my wife Jennifer, and to our five children—Jocelyn, Christopher, Aubrey, Spencer, and Emily. They make life meaningful and enjoyable. Any professional success I might achieve would be empty without them.

PART I

TREK OVERVIEW

Among mountaineers and other connoisseurs of geologic form, Everest is not regarded as a particularly comely peak. Its proportions are too chunky, too broad of beam, too crudely hewn. But what Everest lacks in architectural grace, it makes up for with sheer, overwhelming mass.

—*Jon Krakauer* (Into Thin Air, *pp. 15–16*)

Twenty minutes beyond the village I rounded a bend and arrived at a breathtaking overlook . . . seven thousand feet higher still, dwarfing Ama Dablam, was the icy thrust of Everest itself . . . I stared at the peak for perhaps thirty minutes, trying to apprehend what it would be like to be standing on that gale-swept vertex. Although I'd ascended hundreds of mountains, Everest was so different from anything I'd previously climbed that my powers of imagination were insufficient for the task. The summit looked so cold, so high, so impossibly far away. I felt as though I might as well be on an expedition to the moon. As I turned away to continue walking up the trail, my emotions oscillated between nervous anticipation and a nearly overwhelming sense of dread.

—*Jon Krakauer* (Into Thin Air, *pp. 58–59*)

The emotions shared by Jon Krakauer while looking up at a distant Everest capture effectively the feelings shared by most individuals when dealing with career or job change, particularly new college graduates. Like ascending Mount Everest, choosing a career path or even obtaining a particular job can feel like an overwhelming task. We often view people in extremely successful careers in the same way Krakauer viewed Everest ("so high, so impossibly far away . . ."). The purpose of this book is to provide you with tools and concepts that should make the overwhelming feel attainable.

One of the biggest challenges of career management is narrowing down the possibilities. With any decision in life, we can only select an alternative from

1

among those options with which we are familiar. The Internet allows us to quickly assess many more job opportunities and prospective employers than we ever could before. Although beneficial in many ways, we can easily become overwhelmed with all of the potential paths available. So one of our primary objectives is to make this mountain of career options seem manageable. Rest assured, you can do it.

The first Part of *Career Trek* is intended as an overview of the challenges and exhilaration that await you. Chapter 1 emphasizes three fundamental principles of successful career management that will assist you regardless of your career path. Chapter 2 describes popular career theories and how they have evolved over the years. It also stresses key attitudes, assumptions, and approaches that enhance career success. It ends with a critical principle by Tom Peters that will cause you to start thinking of your career as a brand and managing it accordingly.

Without further ado, it is time for a high-level look at the mountain that awaits you.

Finding Your Fit, Passion, and Smile

DILBERT: © Scott Adams/Dist. by United Feature Syndicate, Inc.

This Dilbert strip illustrates three fundamental concepts that are essential to successful careers, whether in business or in other fields—fit, passion, and a smile (which is an important manifestation of joy and a positive attitude). If the fit is right, people will love their jobs, even jobs that are seen as undesirable by 99% of the population (e.g., the Grim Reaper's vocation). You can see the nonverbal and read the verbal contrast in the attitudes of Dilbert and the Grim Reaper about their respective jobs.

Consider your choice of academic and professional career goals for a minute. To what extent are those goals based on doing what you love to do? To what extent are those goals based on what others tell you are good fields to pursue? Most reports indicate that business professionals spend between 50 and 55 hours per week on work activities. It is not uncommon for managers and executives to work 60 or more hours on a weekly basis. Don't even ask founders of new start-up companies about their work hours. How does 7 days a week, 12 to 18 hours a day sound to you? Even at 50 hours a week, that amount of time meets or more likely exceeds time spent sleeping. Time spent at work typically exceeds quality time spent with family, friends, and other loved ones. Now if you multiply 50 hours per week by 50 weeks per year (remember you get 2 weeks off for the typical paid vacation offered by U.S. companies) by 40 years of full-time employment, then you are talking about 100,000 hours devoted to your employment responsibilities. This point is not made to denigrate the value of work. In fact, hard work is a timeless success factor and an important principle of life. But if we are going to spend such a large portion of our short time on this earth in work-related activities, then we should do something we enjoy, something we feel passionate about, and work that we believe makes a difference. *To reiterate the central message of this chapter, remember the following three principles throughout your career trek*:

1. **Find your fit.**
2. **Pursue your passion.**
3. **Share your smile.**

When you are considering possible career paths or changing jobs, it can be helpful to consider the following questions:

- Will this new opportunity fit better with my skills and aspirations?
- Am I likely to be more or less passionate in this situation?
- Can I see myself feeling and sharing greater joy if I make this choice?

Let's explore these fundamental principles in more depth.

FIND YOUR FIT

Much research shows the value of fit. An extensive study from the Gallup organization involving over 1 million employees and 50,000 managers revealed that one skill that differentiates the best managers from mediocre managers is the ability to place their employees in the right roles to utilize their strongest attributes.[1] In other words, they understand the concept of *person–job fit*. The concept is not difficult to understand but it is quite often overlooked by both employers and employees. Person–job fit means a good match, or alignment, between an individual's characteristics and the attributes of a particular job. The accompanying model depicts the key variables in analyzing person–job fit.

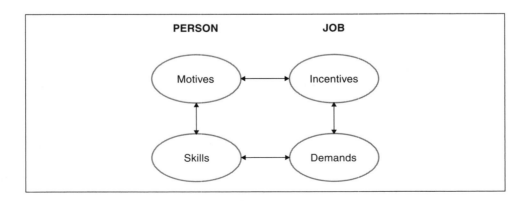

---

[1] Buckingham, M., & Coffman, C. (1999). *First, break all the rules: What the world's greatest managers do differently*. New York: Simon & Schuster.

The Person–Job Fit Model

As you can see in the figure, two sets of characteristics are related to the person and two are related to the job. This model can be used both to examine your fit in a current job and to consider the potential fit in a prospective job opportunity. To properly apply this model, we need to discuss the specifics of each of the model's variables, starting with the person variables.

Motives. What are you looking for in a job, and more broadly, in your career? Your motives are both your aspirations and your values (i.e., what is important to you). The following Trek Task should help you start to identify some of your stronger motives.

 TREK TASK 1

WHAT DO YOU WANT TO BE WHEN YOU GROW UP?

When you were 10 years old or younger, what did you most want to do when you became an adult? What was your vocational aspiration when you finished high school? Finally, if you could do any *one* occupation right now, what would it be? Write your answers and for each one identify two or three reasons why you were (or are) interested in that occupation.

A personal illustration will demonstrate how this activity can help you uncover some of your career motives. I wanted to be a doctor when I was 10, largely because of three factors: (a) I could help people in need, (b) I had an older cousin who just finished medical school and felt a tremendous sense of accomplishment, and (c) the wealth and status accorded to doctors. You may or may not still have aspirations for that desired occupation of your youth. I quit wanting to be a doctor when I realized that I become very squeamish around hospitals, blood, needles, people in pain, and the like. Not a good fit, obviously! But go beyond the simple yes or no answer of your current interest in this occupation. Look at the factors. Are they still important to you? If so, can you prioritize them in order of importance? In my case, helping people was and is my top priority. My current profession allows me to do that on a regular basis. A sense of accomplishment is still important, but instead of becoming a medical doctor, I fulfilled that motive by earning a Ph.D. in business administration. Finally, I learned over time that wealth and status was less crucial to my happiness than I initially thought. After all, I did go into academia, not exactly the industry of millionaires. This is just an example of how to explore your motives. Other methods for examining your career motives will be covered in Chapter 3 (Who Are You?).

Skills. You need to evaluate three main categories of skills—technical/functional, interpersonal, and conceptual. *Technical skills* comprise your capabilities with particular technologies and other job-specific processes related to a company's equipment and products. *Functional skills* relate to understanding and expertise with major business functions (e.g., sales, marketing, operations, finance). These technical/functional skills may have been acquired through formal education and/or work experience, and their competent demonstration is most important in new jobs and in entry-level professional positions.

Interpersonal skills are never unimportant, but they become more essential to your career success as you attain managerial and leadership positions. These skills include both written and verbal communication capabilities. They also encompass skills in conflict resolution and influence tactics. Perhaps the most important of these skills, and the one for which we usually have the most inflated perception of our own prowess, is the skill of effective listening. When David Bennett (a close colleague and former executive of Marriott and Mailboxes, Etc.) and I interviewed executives about their worst decisions, most of them recalled people issues (such as conflict with a business partner, hiring the wrong person, or leaving a poor performer in a job too long before letting that person go). They emphasized how important it is to hone these skills.

The third skill set, often called *conceptual skills*, consists of analytical abilities and the capacity to solve challenging problems, especially those calling for creative solutions. This set of skills also relates to your ability to think strategically and keep the big picture in mind when analyzing data and making decisions. It is important that you know your problem-solving limitations and preferences. How creative are you in your thinking? To what extent do you prefer very structured problems to more ambiguous difficulties? How well do you analyze and solve problems under intense time constraints? Good employers do everything in their power to retain the services of those employees who proactively identify and resolve organizational challenges.

Discovering your strongest skills is the focus of Chapter 4 (What Is in Your Pack?). However, before we leave this topic a couple of other thoughts are in order. First, employers often explicitly state that they want to hire people with good leadership skills. So where are leadership skills in terms of these three categories? Effective leaders draw from all three skill areas. They establish credibility by demonstrating at least a moderate degree of technical/functional skill. They excel in interpersonal skills. And they become very good at conceptual skills, particularly the strategic thinking aspect of that skill set. Second, there is an important yet subtle difference between skills and talents. That distinction will be explained in Chapter 4. Let us now look at the two job variables—demands and incentives.

Demands. This use of the word *demands* does not represent how much employment demand there is for a particular occupation, although that is another factor that you should at least consider in your career decision. In this case, we can broadly define *job demands* as *what you must deliver to meet the expectations for a given position.* One way to start identifying these demands is through the formal job description, provided one exists. Although companies are becoming more specific with their job descriptions, you will likely need to dig well beyond this surface-level information if you want greater clarity of the job's demands. The information you need to know includes usual stress level, hours worked per week, reporting structure (who you report to), nature of key work activities, key internal and/or external customers, team-based or individual focus, working conditions, cultural demands, and rate of change or amount of ambiguity. For any particular job, you must also ask What skills are needed to achieve this job's objectives? and What required qualifications exist for performing in this position?

Incentives. The final component of the Person–Job Fit model is *incentives, or the rewards provided by the company for satisfactory performance of the job's demands.* I tend to group incentives in two categories, monetary and nonmonetary. Key monetary incentives are base salary, bonuses, other benefits in the overall compensation package, and stock option plans. Nonmonetary incentives are much less consistent from job to job and, therefore, usually more difficult to compare. Some common nonmonetary incentives are opportunities for advancement and/or professional growth, freedom and independence, company culture, passion, exciting work, quality coworkers, and opportunities to travel. In today's business environment many companies offer unique incentives (although not as abundantly as in 1999 to 2000, at the height of the dot-com craze). Check some of these out from *Fortune*'s 100 Best Companies annual list:[2]

- MBNA provides up to a $20,000 reimbursement for any employee who adopts a child.
- Texas Instruments offers an in-house spa and occasional on-site driver's license renewals.
- J. M. Smucker serves employees complimentary muffins and bagels every day.
- General Mills reimburses 100 percent of employee tuition (up to $6,000), even for new employees.
- Men's Wearhouse makes a 3-week paid sabbatical available to employees after 5 years.

Personal Illustration of Fit

My decision to change occupations from an information technology (IT) consultant to a business professor illustrates effectively the fit concept. Putting my family first has always been my top priority. Thus, my first career motive is to have the flexibility and independence to balance work and family demands. The only career path in large IT consulting firms at the time was to progress until becoming an associate partner and then a full equity partner in the firm. In my branch office, I noted that a majority of the partners were divorced or had never been married. After considering this, my conclusion was that to be a successful partner your job responsibilities were expected to be your first priority in life. That would not be the case for me. When I was given the opportunity to obtain a Ph.D. and become a business professor, I researched the incentives of such a position and recognized a better fit. Then I investigated the demands of being a professor: conducting research, teaching effectively to different audience levels (undergraduate, MBA, executive MBA), serving on committees, and advising students, to name a few. I believed that other than the research skills, I had the other technical, interpersonal, and conceptual skills to perform well in this occupation. Others who were

---

[2] Levering, R., & Moskowitz, M. (2005, January 4). 100 best companies to work for. *Fortune*, pp. 61–97. This information can also be examined to a lesser extent (for nonsubscribers) at www.fortune.com).

further along in that career path explained that the doctoral program would help me gain sufficient research capabilities to forge a career as a business professor.

Had I stayed with the IT consulting firm, I would be a full equity partner by now and my annual salary would be upward of $300,000, but I would have missed most of my children's school functions, spent considerable time in airports, and worked countless hours of overtime. In my current occupation, I don't have extended out-of-town assignments. During the academic semesters I still work 50 hours per week, but for the most part I pick and choose the times and locations. My family has dinner together practically every night, and my children are acquiring a stronger love for learning. Finally, I love what I do and I look forward each day to my work activities (except for grading—but how many professors enjoy that?). I am not saying that your motives need to be the same as mine. Just make sure that you make career choices that provide a strong fit with your unique motives and skills.

 TREK TASK 2
EVALUATING PERSON–JOB FIT

Using the four components of the Person–Job Fit model previously described, evaluate the fit of your current or most recent job. What one characteristic of the job or the employer, if changed, would most improve the fit?

PURSUE YOUR PASSION

A common dilemma that you will likely face in your career is the question do I follow the money or the passion? Carly Fiorina, former CEO of Hewlett-Packard has said, *"Love what you do. Success requires passion."*[3] It is clear she did not love everything about her five-plus years at HP, but her philosophy has been reinforced by practically every successful executive I have interviewed. In fact, most executives assert that as you follow your passion the money will come. Anne Fisher elaborates on why passion is so important to career success:

> Fun? Do real, live, wildly successful grown-up executives really plan their careers around *fun*? You bet they do—and so should you. There's a practical reason for it: If you don't love what you do, you won't be terrific enough at it to compete against those who do. "The passionate ones are the ones who will go the extra mile, do the extra work, come up with the fresh, outside-the-box idea," says Phyllis Woods, a senior consultant at career-counseling firm Drake Beam Morin in Seattle. "To get ahead today, your first question shouldn't be, Where are the hot jobs now? It should be, What can I get passionate about?"[4]

---

[3] Fiorina, C. (1999, September 29). Making the best of a mess. *New York Times*, p. C8.

[4] Fisher, A. (2001). *If my career's on the fast track, where do I get a road map?* New York: William Morrow, p. 20.

So you need to figure out what activities you truly enjoy and where your passions lie. This is not as easy as it sounds. In my undergraduate program, passion for teaching at the university level was not even on my radar. Most individuals learn what activities they really dislike sooner than those they love. Note the following two caveats about passion.

- *Marry your passion with real skills.* I am extremely passionate about sports and would have loved to become a pro basketball player, a pro football player, or a champion tennis player at Wimbledon. But as Clint Eastwood once said in one of his Dirty Harry films, "A man's got to know his limitations." My athletic skills and height are, shall we say, lacking! Fortunately, most of us have multiple passions in life. The trick is figuring out where passion and skill meet and where others will pay us enough to perform those activities. Of the two—passion and skill—I suggest you start investigating career paths based on passion rather than skill. You can learn new skills easier than you can become passionate about something that doesn't excite you. For example, I was one of the top performers in my college accounting courses, yet I had minimal passion for that field.

- *Realize that unbridled passions can lead to disastrous consequences.* Following your passion without a moral compass or while neglecting contextual changes can be hazardous (ask Enron employees or any number of cutting-edge tech wizards who left Microsoft in the late 1990s to pursue IPO dreams with unsuccessful dot-coms). We can certainly be overzealous in our passions. For example, I love to eat, but if I don't show some self-discipline this passion will lessen my productivity and eventually destroy me physically. As the character John Keating (played by Robin Williams) exclaimed in the film *Dead Poet's Society*, "Sucking the marrow out of life doesn't mean choking on the bone!"

SHARE YOUR SMILE

There has perhaps never been a more important time in our nation's history for people to rediscover their smiles and strive to find true meaning and joy in their lives. In the aftermath of 9/11, the lingering war in Iraq, hurricanes Katrina and Rita, and yes, even rising gasoline prices, there are obviously legitimate causes for concern. But we must not let those external factors rob us of our sense of humor and inner joy. Those of you who have experienced a truly stressful, frustrating, painful day and then have been greeted by the sincere smile of a child know the power of that simple facial expression.

This point about smiling and joy may be received with some cynicism. Is it really necessary? Doesn't it need to be genuine? It sounds too rah-rah, doesn't it? These are legitimate concerns about this topic. When I refer to smiling it is in the context of someone who genuinely exudes positive feelings because they enjoy what they do and their work environment. I am not talking about smiling to give people false impressions. Smiling and joy are natural consequences of the first two principles discussed in this chapter. When your job fit is good and you are largely doing what you love to do, joy is one of the resulting feelings, and it is often manifested in how often you smile during the workday.

To answer the question about whether sharing your smile is really an essential element of career success, please read on and weigh the evidence. Smiling and sharing that smile with others is as much about attitude as anything else. A positive, enthusiastic attitude does wonders for your career success. Consider the following statement about modeling a positive attitude:

> Attitudes most often manifest themselves as judgmental statements expressing personal feelings. It is not unusual for an attitude to be translated into a behavior. The manner in which you present yourself and your response to various situations frequently set the stage for success. Often, what is said is not as important as how it is communicated and the accompanying nonverbal signals. The most prevalent nonverbal cues to attitude are facial expressions. The face and the eyes tell all. Many people fail to realize that they continually send emotional messages through facial expressions. Displaying a continual frown, wrinkling of the brow, or sighing is interpreted as an expression of anxiety and tension. The message delivered is "things are just not going well." On the other hand, a sincere smile is a powerful tool for communicating a positive attitude. It does not cost a cent, it makes you feel better, it helps prevent facial lines, and it is reassuring to others. However, do not overdo it. Continually smiling during inappropriate situations may result in your being either institutionalized or investigated by internal security.[5]

Kevin and Jackie Freiberg take this principle a step further. They are business consultants and authors of the book *Nuts!* about Southwest Airlines. In their most recent book, entitled *Guts!*, they devote an entire chapter to the importance of hiring people with good humor and positive attitudes. The chapter is "Gutsy Leaders Hire People Who Don't Suck."[6] Read their explanation of this provocative principle:

> There are people who can find opportunity in any adversity. Good-humored and optimistic, they make life fun. They inspire enthusiasm and are willing to try new things. And we're all better for having them around. Then there are people who can find the difficulty in every opportunity. They are cynical, sarcastic, and pessimistic. They hate what they do and complain about everything. They sap our energy, and we gain nothing from their presence. Which kind of person do you want to hire? We think the answer is obvious. Moose Millard, a dear friend of ours, once said, "Bad attitudes suck! They suck the passion, energy, teamwork, unity, and life right out of your organization." That's why the strategic hiring philosophy of nearly every gutsy leader we know is to hire people who don't suck.[7]

A strong visual reminder of the link between smiling and career success is found in the saga of Mitchie the Kid, from the movie *City Slickers*. Career and organizational consultants Dick Leider and David Shapiro wrote an excellent synopsis of this film that hits straight to the current point.

---

[5] Scarnati, J. T. (2002). Leaders as role models: 12 rules. *Career Development International*: Vol. 7 (3, pp. 181–189).

[6] Freiberg, K., & Freiberg, J. (2004). *Guts!* New York: Texere, pp. 111–151.

[7] Ibid., pp. 111–112.

Billy Crystal plays Mitch Robbins, a disillusioned radio advertising salesperson who takes a much-needed vacation at a western dude ranch with a couple of long-time friends. At the beginning of the film, he considers whether he really wants to go— what with the daily trials and tribulations of his life, he thinks the trip will be more trouble than it's worth. His wife disagrees, explaining why she thinks it's so necessary that he get away.

"You need to go find your smile," she tells him. She insists that rediscovering his sense of humor matters more than anything else he's doing at the time.

She's right. And over the course of the film, Mitch learns this too. He comes to understand the value of laughter and what a difference it makes to have a smile in one's heart. At the end of the movie, nothing in his life has changed, but everything has. He still has the same job, the same family, the same problems, but having refound his smile, is able to embrace them with a renewed sense of joy.[8]

How many of us feel like Mitch? Have you lost your smile and your joy in life? Experiments reported by author Gordon Wainwright revealed that changing posture and increased smiling resulted in greater respect, being taken more seriously, and being treated more positively by coworkers.[9] A former CEO of a career consulting company shared with me and my careers students two primary reasons why employers will hire you: (a) they think you will make them money, and (b) they like you. It is much easier to be liked by others if you smile and demonstrate at least a modest sense of humor. This is especially true if you are able to laugh at yourself and not take yourself too seriously. We all know people who are a bit too full of themselves. Of course, this is coming from someone who willingly shows his students an eighth-grade photo of himself with a full-blown afro hairstyle (very scary!). One more thing, joy and fun are not synonymous. "For many people, 'fun' has become an addiction. But as with most addictive substances, people build up a tolerance to it. So despite all the 'fun' things people do, they're still not having fun. What's really missing is a sense of joy."[10]

Think about that distinction for a moment. How many "fun" activities do we have to choose from? When we lived in Southern California, my family and I were within 90 minutes of Disneyland, Disney's California Adventure, SeaWorld, Legoland, the San Diego Zoo, the San Diego Wild Animal Park, Knotts Berry Farm, and Universal Studios. So the area offered ample opportunities for fun. And yet, how many depressed, unhappy people did we encounter on a typical day? We could attribute some of that unhappiness to crowded freeways, economic concerns, or seeing their favorite *American Idol* singer voted off, but not that much of it. Fun is fleeting, joy is enduring. Fun tends to be centered on what we do and on things. Joy has much more to do with who we are, with the quality of our most important relationships, and with a recognition that we are making a positive difference in the lives of others.

The bottom line is that you need to consider and explore jobs that will fit both your motives and your skills. Don't expect your first job to be your ideal job, but neither should it be a poor or even a mediocre fit. Figure out your most marketable

[8] Leider, R. J., & Shapiro, D. A. (1996). *Repacking your bags.* San Francisco: Berrett Koehler Publishers, p. 10.

[9] Wainwright, G. (2003). *Teach yourself body language.* Upper Saddle River, NJ: Prentice Hall.

[10] Leider & Shapiro, p. 11.

passions. And don't lose your smile along this challenging, unpredictable career journey. With these three principles—**find your fit, pursue your passion, share your smile**—firmly in tow, it is time to head toward base camp to take a good look at the mountain that awaits us.

TREK LIST

- ☐ **FIND YOUR FIT.**   I understand the relationship between the two person variables (motives and skills) and the two job variables (demands and incentives) in the Person–Job Fit model.
- ☐ **PURSUE YOUR PASSION.**   I have started to think about what I enjoy doing the most and what types of careers might allow me to perform those activities on a regular basis.
- ☐ **SHARE YOUR SMILE.**   I am considering how I can increase the level of joy in my life, as well as how my verbal and nonverbal expressions reflect my attitude to those around me.

Destination
A Successful Career

2

Success consists of going from failure to failure without loss
of enthusiasm.

—*Winston Churchill*

Not to dampen your enthusiasm about the trek ahead of you, but we all
make mistakes along the way to a successful career. Bob McRann,
former general manager of Cox Communications in San Diego, was
asked how he tried to balance the professional and personal demands in his
career. He indicated that early in his career he didn't, and it cost him his first
marriage. He then told our students, *"You have to decide whether you are the
type who works to live or the type who lives to work"* (emphasis added).
You will experience some failures as you ascend the career mountain.
However, if you are passionate about what you do and a good person–job fit
exists, your enthusiasm should not wane, as Churchill emphasized in the
chapter-opening quote.

For you to effectively manage your career, it is essential that you keep clearly
in mind what constitutes a successful career to you. At the end of this chapter
I have included a brief self-assessment survey that scholars use when they
research perceptions of career success. Just remember that neither these
survey items nor I can tell you with certainty how you should define career
success. Only you can decide that. And as it did for Bob McRann, your view
of career success may change over time. Thinking about it now is an important start for your career journey. The definition may not be as simple as
"I work to live" or "I live to work." Do the following exercise and write down
your thoughts.

TREK TASK 3

RETIREMENT SPEECH

You are preparing your retirement speech. You reflect upon your career. What do you hope you can say about your career? What indicators will tell you that your career was successful? What regrets do you absolutely want to avoid?

THE MOUNTAIN AWAITS

Refining your personal definition of career success will determine the summit of the mountain you are trying to reach. While you are grappling with this success definition, it is important to understand a few realities of Mount Career as it stands today. Natural mountains in our world are not static, not by a long shot. They just seem that way most of the time because they typically change very slowly over hundreds and thousands of years, barring major natural phenomena (earthquakes, floods) and manmade interventions. Mount Career has changed much more visibly and rapidly over time. The following shifts have occurred in the past 200 years.

TIME PERIOD	CAREER CHARACTERISTICS
1800–1870	Agricultural, trade/craftsmen
1870–1945	Business owner, factory worker, artisan
1945–1990	Organization man, climb the ladder
1990–present	Free agents, protean, boundaryless, turbulent

Brief Overview of Career Development Theories

It is beneficial for you to understand some frameworks for thinking about your evolving career. Over the past 50 years, the following theories (or models) of career development have been prominently discussed:

- Trait-factor theory
- Developmental/career stage theories
- Personality typology theory
- Protean/boundaryless career perspective

Trait-Factor Theory. Frank Parsons first conceptualized the idea of "careers" almost 100 years ago. He claimed that career success was largely dependent upon three factors: (a) accurate knowledge of self; (b) accurate knowledge of job specifications; and (c) the ability to match up individual traits with job require-ments.[1] This should sound familiar to you because it formed the roots of the Person–Job Fit model described in Chapter 1. This approach became known as the trait-factor theory of career development. The key assumption of this theory is that closely matched individual traits and job factors result in career success and satisfaction. This fundamental notion is still prominent today.

Developmental or Career Stages Theories. These theories present careers in a more dynamic light and suggest that career choices vary over time based on individual maturity and career stage. Two popular models that describe these developmental changes are the Life-Span/Life-Space model by Donald Super[2] and the Professional Career Stages model developed by Gene Dalton and Paul Thompson.[3] Super's model is based on the self-concept, or our knowledge of who we are, and how that evolves over time and is related to our career choices. He identified the following five vocational development stages.

VOCATIONAL DEVELOPMENT STAGE	AGE	CHARACTERISTICS
Crystallization	14–18	Developing a tentative vocational goal
Specification	18–21	Firming up the vocational goal
Implementation	21–24	Training for and obtaining employment
Stabilization	24–35	Working and confirming vocational choice
Consolidation	35+	Focusing on career advancement

Dalton and Thompson's model was developed from research with engineers, lawyers, and accountants, and was therefore termed the Professional Career Stages model. They identified the following four stages and related issues and activities.

	STAGE I	STAGE II	STAGE III	STAGE IV
Central activity	Learning to work and follow directions	Independent contributor	Training and managing others	Shaping the direction of the organization
Primary relationship	Apprentice	Colleagues	Mentor	Sponsor
Major psychological issues	Dependence	Independence	Assuming responsibility for others	Exercising power and influence

[1] Parsons, F. (1909). *Choosing a vocation.* New York: Agathon Press.

[2] Super, D. E. (1990). A life-span, life-space approach to career development. In D. Brown & L. Brooks (Eds.), *Career choice and development: Applying contemporary theories to practice* (2nd ed.). San Francisco: Jossey-Bass.

[3] Dalton, G. W., & Thompson, P. H. (1986). *Novations: Strategies for career management.* Glenview, IL: Scott Foresman and Company.

The drawback to both of these models is that they were developed when individual careers were more stable and people stayed in a single vocation for all or most of their working lives. In the current environment, individuals are more likely to go through these developmental and professional stages multiple times as they change careers. The information revolution also allows individuals to pass through these stages much more quickly than when these models were studied and developed.

Personality Typology Theory. Perhaps the most well known of any career theory is John Holland's personality typology theory.[4] Holland's central premise is that people choose careers based on compatibility with their dominant personality characteristics. From his lengthy research in this area, he has identified the following six common personality types.

PERSONALITY TYPE	BASIC ATTRIBUTES
Realistic	Prefers working with things; sees self as practical and hands-on learner
Investigative	Prefers working with ideas and solving quantitative problems; sees self as intellectual
Artistic	Prefers creative activities; sees self as expressive and independent
Social	Prefers working with and helping people; sees self as friendly and trusting
Enterprising	Prefers to lead and influence others; sees self as energetic and ambitious
Conventional	Prefers to work with data; sees self as structured and organized

Most people have a few dominant personality types, and Holland asserts that career success is more likely when individuals engage in occupations that have greater consistency with their most prominent personality characteristics.

The Protean or Boundaryless Career. The most recent shift in the terrain of Mount Career is instructive and deserving of our attention. The change has been from an organizational career (driven and managed by the company, with an implied promise of long-term employment and progressive promotions up the company's hierarchy) to what Hall termed over 25 years ago the protean career.[5]

The protean career is derived from the name of Proteus, a Greek god who was believed to be able to change shape whenever he desired. Most careers experts today suggest that the average American will have three to five different *careers* (not jobs, but careers) over the full course of their working lives. The protean

---

[4] Holland, J. W.; also see www.careerkey.org for more information and practical applications of Holland's theory.

[5] Hall, D. T. (1976). *Careers in organizations.* Glenview, IL: Scott, Foresman.

career definition aptly describes the shifts that may occur as individuals pursue psychological success and personal fulfillment in their careers. A more formal definition of this career concept is provided by Hall:

> The protean career is a process which the person, not the organization, is managing. It consists of all the person's varied experiences in education, training, work in several organizations, changes in occupational field, etc. The protean career is *not* what happens to the person in any one organization. The protean person's own personal choices and search for self-fulfillment are the unifying or integrative elements in his or her life. The criterion of success is internal (psychological success), not external. In short, the protean career is shaped more by the individual than by the organization and may be redirected from time to time to meet the needs of the person.[6]

The intent of this section was not to offer a thorough critique or analysis of career theories. Instead, the purpose was to orient you to different frameworks that have been commonly used to understand career development activities.[7]

Becoming a Career Activist

Perhaps the most important implication of the protean career is that you must take charge of managing your career. You should not leave that activity in the hands of any organization. You must become what Dr. Barbara Moses termed a *career activist*. She clarifies this concept as "defining yourself independently from your organization, and taking charge of your own career choices."[8] Even working with the best companies doesn't ensure that "they've got your back," so to speak, when it comes to your career. Organizations tend to protect their business interests first and employee career needs come later. Nor does high individual performance guarantee that you will have a secure future within a given company. A friend of mine shared a personal experience when he was let go from a metal-stamping company. He had been their top salesperson and exceeded his annual quota so much that the company determined they had sufficient contracts to keep them busy for a couple of years. They no longer wanted to pay his large commissions and so they pushed him out the door. If you believe this was an unfair outcome for my friend, I would absolutely concur. But for my friend, those few months of unemployment were a time to become a career activist and take charge of his career direction. He leveraged his passion for surfing and his desire to be his own boss and started a small business—a surf and skateboard shop. The challenge is great as he strives to establish a successful business, but he loves what he does.

In addition to being a career activist, Moses cites three other key principles for managing one's career.[9] These principles point to the end result of psychological

---

[6] Ibid., p. 201 (quoted in Hall & Mirvis, 1996).

[7] If more thorough analysis of career theories is desired, I recommend two books: (1) *Handbook of career counseling theory and practice* (1996), edited by M. L. Savickas and W. B. Walsh, Palo Alto, CA: Davies-Black Publishing; and (2) *Handbook of career theory* (1989), edited by M. B. Arthur, D. T. Hall, & B. S. Lawrence, New York: Cambridge University Press.

[8] Moses, B. (1997). *Career intelligence*. San Francisco: Berrett-Koehler Publishers, p. 138.

[9] Ibid., p. 138.

career success mentioned in Hall's definition of the protean career. The three principles are:

1. Know yourself (your aspirations, strengths, what you have to offer).
2. Know what you love.
3. Be who you are.

I hope you recognize already that self-awareness is critical to your pursuit of a successful career. It is essential to the fit issue described in the previous chapter. It influences what you choose to include and not include on your résumé. It is vital to your ability to interview effectively. More often than not, interviewers will ask you a question or two about your strengths and weaknesses. Self-awareness helps you learn what opportunities to say yes to, and which ones to politely but firmly avoid. I will help you increase your self-awareness in the next few chapters. For now, it is sufficient that you see the clear connection between self-awareness and being a career activist. The stronger you know yourself, the more you can confidently take charge of your career and its key decisions.

Dr. Moses adds that becoming a career activist involves at least these four activities:

1. Writing your own script rather than waiting for someone else to write it for you
2. Being vigilant in identifying and preparing for opportunities
3. Thinking of yourself as an independent agent, in terms and concepts that are independent of your position title, your company, or the perceptions of others about your job
4. Being entrepreneurial, seeking opportunities (with their associated risks)[10]

We have established that the mountain awaiting your climb—Mount Career—is best navigated when you are proactively managing your ascent up the mountain. It is like the commercials of a few years ago for Volkswagen, the popular automobile manufacturer. The slogan was "Drivers wanted." The same call goes out in the career trek, "Drivers wanted." Take the wheel of your career! Don't leave your employer at the wheel.

This does not mean that you should not care about what organizations offer in terms of career development. The best companies recognize that individuals want to continually grow and increase their marketability. One good source for such companies is *Fortune's* annual "100 Best Companies to Work For" issue. Another is to look at your current (or prospective) employer and answer a few basic questions. How much value do they place on employee development? Who owns the career development activities, HR or the line managers? How much time and resources are committed to training and development costs? It's not that you want to turn the wheel of your career vehicle over to the organization, but good organizations can provide additional fuel, help keep the car well maintained, and even offer some upgrades for more effective performance.

---

[10] Ibid., p. 144.

Having established that you need to be in charge of your career development, we now consider the attitudes, assumptions, and approaches related to success (and failure) on this journey. Keep in mind as you read the following section that Dick Bolles, author of the most widely read career help book of all time, *What Color Is Your Parachute?*, once described our typical job-hunting system as Neanderthal.[11]

ATTITUDES, ASSUMPTIONS, AND APPROACHES

Career decisions are among the most important we make in our lives. If we are to make effective decisions on the mountain, we must understand some assumptions about the career trek—both our own assumptions and those of others. Many approaches have also been identified by various experts about how to search for jobs and how to choose a career path. But first, we need to focus on attitude because your attitude about your unfolding career makes all the difference.

Attitude Determines Altitude

One of the points made by Krakauer about the attempts to scale Everest is that the effort is both physically and mentally excruciating. This is an activity where one poor decision, one mental miscalculation can be fatal. So it is with your career. Scaling professional heights is usually time-consuming, and there is no substitute for hard work. And yet, the distinguishing factor between those who obtain career success and those who do not is frequently a matter of attitude. Just like on Everest, in your pursuit of the career summit, your attitude determines your altitude.

How do you feel in general about your potential for a successful career? Is it a sure thing? Is it a strong possibility? Is it possible, but only if you get a few breaks along the way? Is it in doubt? Is it never going to happen? A positive attitude about your career is a good thing, there is no question about that. However, this isn't just a Stuart Smalley exercise in positive talk and self-esteem.[12] You can't just look in the mirror and exclaim, "I'm smart and I like myself," and call that a positive attitude about your career.

What manifestations of your attitude are employers looking for? They want to see *energy and enthusiasm*, first and foremost. You know people who are always negative, with the proverbial "cloud raining on my parade" type of attitude. Remember the Freibergs' principle, "Hire people who don't suck." In a guest appearance in my class, Kevin Freiberg explained that you don't want to bring people into your culture who suck the energy and life out of the organization because of their negative attitudes. Instead, your enthusiasm should inject life and positive energy into others, propelling the organization toward exceeding its goals.

---

[11] Bolles, R. N. (2001). *What color is your parachute?* Berkeley, CA: Ten Speed Press, p. 10.

[12] From the TV series *Saturday Night Live* character Stuart Smalley played by Al Franken. See also Franken, A. (1992). *I'm good enough, I'm smart enough, and doggone it, people like me! Daily affirmations by Stuart Smalley.* New York: Dell.

A second aspect of attitude that is important is how you *react to change and deal with adversity*. We live in a very turbulent social climate, and that is reflected in an uncertain economy and constantly changing business environments. When things go wrong, are you the first to point fingers at others? Or do you look to your own performance for possible improvements? A final dimension of our attitudes is commonly referred to by hiring managers as *"can do" attitude*. Helen Adams, a partner in the accounting firm Deloitte & Touche, said that you should never turn down an assignment "because it isn't part of my formal job requirements." Companies are looking for people who identify problems and resolve them rather than waiting to be told to fix the problem. Employers look for a proactive approach by employees that shows they want to make the company better rather than just doing the minimum work needed to earn a paycheck. This "can do" attitude helps give us courage to take a few steps beyond our comfort zones and tackle new challenges, thereby developing new skills and expertise in the process.

How important is attitude to your job success? One author argues that employers should "hire for attitude, train for skill."[13] The rationale behind his argument is that who we are (including our attitude) doesn't change much over time and is extremely difficult for an employer to change, but both personal effort and company-offered training can develop our skills with relative ease. Remember why employers will hire you: to make them money and because they like you. It is largely your attitude that will determine in an interview whether or not the interviewer likes you. Layoffs and career mistakes may make it difficult to maintain these career-enhancing attitudes, but remember that you have unique talents and you *will* succeed with the right fit.

Common Assumptions

Assumptions are those ideas or perceptions that we believe to be true without a full certainty of their accuracy. For example, I assume that students pursue business degrees because they believe that business provides more financially lucrative career opportunities than a degree in English or history. The lesson is that we need to be careful about our career assumptions. Some possible assumptions to think about include:

- I wouldn't be happy if I relocated outside of my current location.
- I need to choose a career that uses my current degree (or major).
- There aren't any good jobs right now because of the economy.
- Companies won't hire me because I don't have enough full-time work experience.

Of these previous assumptions, the third is blatantly faulty—there are good jobs out there. Even in 2003 there were available positions, despite what the *New York Times* called the "worst hiring slump in 20 years."[14] Relevant majors and

---

[13] Carbonara, P. (1996). Hire for attitude, train for skill. *Fast Company 4*, pp. 73–80.

[14] Leonhardt, D. (2003, February 6). U.S. economy in worst hiring slump in 20 years. *New York Times*.

full-time work experience are certainly helpful factors in obtaining jobs, but they are not entirely necessary. As for the first assumption, if you have never lived outside of your current location, how do you know for sure? The point about assumptions is that we often make decisions without doing any due diligence to gather data that could prove or disprove those assumptions.

Bolles identifies three *fatal job-hunting assumptions* that you should be aware of:

1. "The job-hunter should remain somewhat loose (i.e., vague) about what he or she wants to do, so they will be able to take advantage of whatever vacancies may become available." Especially in the tough job market of the past few years, being more specific and focused in your target will improve your chances for employment. Employers want people who really want *this* job, not just *any* job. Bolles adds, "If you don't state just exactly what you want to do, first of all to yourself, and then to the employers you meet, you are—in effect—handing over that decision to others." So when you refine your résumé and construct your search strategy, be as specific as possible about the occupation, industry, and even job that you want.

2. "The job-hunter should spend his or her time only on those organizations which have already indicated they have a vacancy." Once again, this tendency to focus on known vacancies greatly limits our options. And because so many other job seekers adhere to this assumption, the competition for those known vacancies is stiff. Success is more likely for two other types of positions—unknown vacancies and created vacancies. Unknown vacancies are openings in companies that are not public knowledge, not posted on the company's Web site or Monster.com, nor advertised in the newspapers. Networking plays a crucial role in alerting you to unknown vacancies that fit your skills and specific career objectives. Created vacancies are positions that an organization custom builds for *you*. If you demonstrate passion and knowledge about a company and have a unique mix of talents that an employer needs, then that employer will often figure out a way to hire you, even if your skills mix doesn't really match any existing openings. In this case, you usually face no competition, and that is a beautiful scenario in which to find yourself.

3. "Employers only see people who can write well."[15] This final assumption relates to the prominence of résumé mailing (and online résumé posting) as the common approach to finding a job. If your résumé is not written well, regardless of your other talents, it is very likely that you may not receive an interview. Again, if you use a different approach to obtain an interview—through networking, for example—then the written quality of your résumé becomes less of a factor.

---

[15] Bolles, R. N., pp. 51–52.

Career Approaches

As I hope you have picked up on, some of the dominant career assumptions have surfaced because of largely ineffective approaches to job and career searches. The three most common approaches individuals take to try to find a job are sending out résumés, answering newspaper or Internet job ads, and using employment agencies. Statistics indicate that these are three of the least effective approaches, ranging from 5 to about a 28% success rate.[16] Two much more effective approaches that I subscribe to are networking and the targeted approach. The two approaches are largely intertwined. With the targeted approach (named the life-changing job hunt by Bolles), you really focus on *what, where,* and *how.*

- *What* talents, skills, and traits do you have to offer to the world?
- *Where* do you want to offer them? (location, industry, type of organization)
- *How* do you access those organizations that give you the chance to do what you do best?

Networking really comes into play with the how component, but input from valuable members of your network can also help you identify the what and the where. We will go into networking in more depth in Chapter 6. For now, think about who you trust and who has already shown an active interest in supporting you in your career endeavors. Now that you understand some of the attitudes, assumptions, and approaches pertaining to Mount Career, there is one more vital concept that you need to learn before we begin base camp—brand *you.*

BRAND YOU

Tom Peters wrote a provocative article several years ago titled, "The Brand Called You." He likened our careers to managing brands. The conclusion he renders that I fully endorse is that

> Regardless of age, regardless of position, regardless of the business we happen to be in, all of us need to understand the importance of branding. We are CEOs of our own companies: Me Inc. To be in business today, our most important job is to be head marketer for the brand called You.
> It's that simple—and that hard. And that inescapable.[17]

If you feel a little uncomfortable thinking about yourself as a brand, you're not alone. In fact, in your interactions with others, please don't treat them as brands, as you would a company's product. However, in terms of managing our careers, principles of brand management make sense. Why is branding so important to career success? Because as Peters asserts, "The brand is a promise of the value you'll receive."[18] Applicants receive offers from employers because of their potential contribution, not because of past efforts. Just like with products and

---

[16] Bolles, R. N. (2005), pp. 37–38.
[17] Peters, T. (1997). The brand called you. *Fast Company 10*, p. 83.
[18] Ibid.

services, you need to concern yourself with two key brand concepts—brand meaning and brand awareness.

Brand meaning consists of the reputation of your brand, or those characteristics that come to the minds of your coworkers, bosses, direct reports, customers, network contacts, and so on. *Brand awareness* is how well known your brand is in the marketplace (substitute organization, class, professional community, etc.). One of your first career trek tasks is to discover what your brand's message is, so let's follow the process Peters suggests. First, ask yourself these questions and then perform the task below:[19]

- What do I do that I am most proud of?
- What have I accomplished that I can unabashedly brag about?
- What do I want to be famous for?

TREK TASK 4

BRAND YOU STATEMENT

In 15 words or less, capture your unique brand. What do you offer that is different from others or unique? How do you add value to the organizations in which you belong? Remember: 15 words at the most! Play with it and refine it.

Having fun yet? If you are still struggling to develop a captivating and encompassing brand statement, don't worry! The next couple of chapters should help as you explore your career aspirations and best skills. The key is that your brand statement needs to articulate how you contribute value consistently to the organizations with which you work. So that you know that this process is possible, the following is my brand statement:

Developing innovative courses, providing students with a personal touch and bridges to the business community.

What are you known for, and do those items match the brand's intended focus? In my case, I was best known at Cal State San Marcos for two innovative courses—In the Executive's Chair and Career Development—that brought the business community to our students and prepared our students for their transition to that community. What about the personal touch? I know students by name at the end of our first class meeting and will call students by name throughout the semester. My family brings Krispy Kreme doughnuts to the first class meeting. I have held barbecues at my house for senior project teams. My special blend of homemade root beer (no, it doesn't contain 11 secret herbs and spices)

---

[19] Ibid., pp. 84.

was served at the conclusion of the Executive's Chair class (food seems to be a common theme with me). And yes, I show students a photo of my afro hairstyle in 8th grade. None of these personal touches would fully compensate for poor teaching skills, poor course designs, or ineffective communication skills. But they do distinguish me from my many excellent colleagues. A primary purpose of this book is to help you develop Brand You and how you can best leverage your unique capabilities for a successful career.

I encourage you to read the entire Peters article, but as we conclude this chapter, here are a few other key principles from his article to ponder:

- Branding campaigns usually start with increased visibility (to raise brand awareness).
- Everything you choose to do (and choose not to do) communicates your brand's focus.
- Packaging counts.
- Word-of-mouth marketing is the key to personal branding (let others toot your horn).
- Using influence power effectively is critical to growing your brand.
- Write your own career mission statement as CEO of Me, Inc. and review it every few months to see if it still accurately describes your target direction.[20]

Now that I have you thinking about yourself as a brand, we are ready to hike several thousand feet up the mountain to spend significant time on the trek fundamentals. Get ready for base camp!

▲🥾 TREK LIST

☐ **DEFINE CAREER SUCCESS.**   I have developed a working definition of what career success means to me.

☐ **CAREER FRAMEWORKS.**   I understand the central ideas of trait-factor, developmental, personality typology, and protean career approaches.

☐ **CAREER ACTIVIST.**   I am becoming a career activist (i.e., taking control of my career) by increasing my self-awareness, discovering what I love to do, and being myself.

☐ **THREE As.**   I know how attitudes, assumptions, and approaches relate to the career development process.

☐ **BRAND YOU.**   I have created a statement of 15 words or less that captures my unique brand message.

---

[20] Ibid., pp. 84–87.

SELF-ASSESSMENT
(PERCEIVED CAREER SUCCESS SURVEY)

Respond to each item as candidly as possible by circling the number that most closely represents your perceptions of how successful your career has been to the present time.

Item	Not very successful				Very successful
1. How successful has your career been?	1	2	3	4	5
2. Compared to your coworkers, how successful is your career?	1	2	3	4	5
3. How successful do your significant others feel your career has been?	1	2	3	4	5

	Behind		On		Ahead
4. Given your age, do you feel career is on schedule, or ahead or behind schedule?	1	2	3	4	5

As you answered these four questions, what indicators of success did you use to determine the most appropriate level of success?

Source: Turban, D. B., & Dougherty, T. W. (1994). Role of protégé personality in receipt of mentoring and career success. *Academy of Management Journal, 37*(3), 688–702.

PART II

BASE CAMP

A couple of miles farther, the glacier made a sharp turn to the east, we plodded to the crest of a long slope, and spread before us was a motley city of nylon domes. More than three hundred tents . . . speckled the boulder-strewn ice. It took us twenty minutes to locate our compound among the sprawling settlement. As we climbed the final rise, Rob [Krakauer's guide, Rob Hall] strode down to greet us. "Welcome to Everest Base Camp," he grinned. The altimeter on my wristwatch read 17,600 feet.

—*Jon Krakauer* (Into Thin Air, *pp. 75–76*)

Time to get you acclimatized for your future ascent attempts up the mountain toward your career summit. The ascent requires a polished résumé, excellent interviewing skills, and a thorough understanding of the route (or routes) that you plan to take to make your way to the summit. The purpose of base camp is to help you learn the fundamentals for your future climb. Base camp objectives will only be fulfilled if you come out of the experience with a better understanding of two things—yourself and the most appealing routes (career paths) up the mountain.

Just knowing and practicing base camp fundamentals—self-awareness, résumé and cover letter writing, networking, and career path research—will give you an advantage over many individuals who pay minimal attention to these items. However, as the opening quote shows, base camp is a relatively crowded place. What you have to do is prepare yourself to outshine all those other applicants trying to reach similar summits. That ambitious objective requires your best efforts here at base camp.

In the next few chapters, you will explore the following aspects about yourself:

- Career aspirations, personality characteristics, values, and work preferences (Chapter 3)
- Talents and skills, as well as weaknesses (Chapter 4)

- Packaging yourself in the most effective way through your résumés and cover letters (Chapter 5)
- Members of your traveling party, also known as your network (Chapter 6)

To ascend Mount Everest there are three possible routes, depending on the country and side of Everest from which you start the journey. Crossing from one route to another is a physical impossibility at the present time. So once you have selected a starting point, it is critical for all climbers pursuing that route to research it in detail. They need to know every pass, tricky climb, and potential hazard along the route. In like manner, there are three broad career paths that are the most common for college students. After having enhanced your self-awareness, you will then learn about these three paths and the various resources and strategies for researching them. The three paths are

- The corporate path (Chapter 7)
- The entrepreneurial path (Chapter 8)
- The graduate program path (Chapter 8)

Welcome to the Career Trek Base Camp! (What altitude is your wristwatch reading?)

Who Are You?
Career Aspirations and Preferences

3

DILBERT: © Scott Adams/Dist. by United Feature Syndicate, Inc.

The first key activity of base camp is quite possibly the toughest, at least initially. This is especially true for younger trekkers and/or those with less full-time work experience. The wisdom of life and work opportunities typically offer new insights about what makes us tick and who we are. So the first step is to discern our true motives regarding our careers. There are four categories of career motives that we need to explore:

1. *Aspirations.* What should you do with your life? (also addresses career dreams)
2. *Values.* What work-related and personal values are most important to you?
3. *Environment.* What are your work environment preferences?
4. *Personality.* What careers does your personality fit the best?

ASPIRATIONS

Carpe Diem

The message that Mr. Keating (played by Robin Williams) gave to his students in the film *Dead Poets Society* is the message that I repeat to you: Carpe diem! Seize the day! Do you have any dreams about your future? As you look at your résumé, what do you hope to see on it in 3 years? Next year? How about in 10 years? Accounts of successful businesspersons who followed their dreams are abundant (consider Steve Jobs of Apple or Mary Kay Ash of Mary Kay Cosmetics). A compelling example is that of Walt Disney. He turned his dream for creating happy environments for children and families into reality and built the Disney empire, including the commercial icon for children's happiness, Disneyland. Two other true stories of pursuing career dreams despite the loud criticisms of others are found in the films *Rudy* and *The Rookie. Rudy* chronicles the inspiring story of Daniel "Rudy" Ruettiger in his quest to play college football at Notre Dame despite his diminished stature and minimal athletic ability (those attributes remind me of someone!). *The Rookie* is about Jim Morris, a high school teacher and baseball coach who risked injury and, in his late 30s, was successful in a second opportunity to become a major league baseball pitcher.

In both cases, Rudy and Jim endured hardships, doubted occasionally whether or not they would fulfill their dreams, persisted because of their beliefs in the dream, and eventually were recognized because they beat the odds. Note that I am not advocating that you must have a career-related dream or vision at this point in your life. I have several dreams related to my family and spiritual aspects of my life. Becoming a university professor was not a career dream for me. In fact, I was never overly concerned about the content of my career, other than that I wanted to enjoy my work and earn a sufficient income to provide for my wife and future children. Now that I am in this profession, tenure and status are not my dreams. My dreams have been related to projects that I create and see to fruition . . . like my career development course, this book, and the course "In the Executive's Chair," which David Bennett and I created.

All I am suggesting here is that you consider your dreams. Don't ignore what your gut or your heart has been softly urging you to pursue. As the following activity suggests, your aspirations need not be exclusive to occupational pursuits. I have worked with students whose aspirations were to work with Nike or Nordstrom, or who loved the advertising industry. The key is to identify any recurring dreams and to pay attention to them.

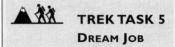 **TREK TASK 5**

DREAM JOB

Do you have a dream job or career? If so, is it specific to a particular company, industry, or occupation? How well do you know what it takes to get started in that job or career? Write down your thoughts.

Po Bronson, author of the book *What Should I Do with My Life? The True Story of People Who Answered the Ultimate Question,* offered the following insights:

> The previous era of business was defined by the question, Where's the opportunity? I'm convinced that business success in the future starts with the question, What should I do with my life? . . . Asking The Question is nothing short of an act of courage: It requires a level of commitment and clarity that is almost foreign to our working lives.[1]

I agree with Bronson except for the assertion that this question is the ultimate question. Other questions related to the purpose of life are more important, but those questions are for another book. What should I do with my life? is a critical question to the career trek for which you are preparing.

Bronson gained two significant insights about answering this question from researching more than 900 life stories of very diverse individuals across the country. The first was that there are no universal categories of "cool" and "uncool" jobs (remember the Grim Reaper in the Dilbert strip). In other words, job demand forecasts can't give you the answer to this question, nor can friends or family. They may help you toward the answer, but in the end, the choice of fulfilling careers is as diverse as the individuals in them. Bronson's second insight is best offered in his own words:

> Your calling isn't something you inherently "know," some kind of destiny. Far from it. Almost all of the people I interviewed found their calling after great difficulty. They had made mistakes before getting it right. . . . Everyone discovered latent talents that weren't in their skill sets at age 25. Most of us don't get epiphanies. We only get a whisper—a faint urge. That's it. That's the call. It's up to you to do the work of discovery, to connect it to an answer.[2]

I agree on this second point completely, for that's how I discovered this "calling." Time for the work of discovery to begin in full earnest, if it has not already.

THE CSMQ

To help you clarify your career aspirations and achieve a more successful person-job fit, I have included an assessment tool called the Career Success Map Questionnaire (CSMQ) at the end of this chapter. This tool was developed in the mid-1980s by Dr. Brooke Derr, global business and careers scholar. *Before you read any further,* turn to the CSMQ and take the assessment.

---

[1] Bronson, P. (January 2003). What should I do with my life? The real meaning of success—and how to find it. *Fast Company,* p. 72.

[2] Ibid., p. 75.

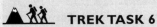

TREK TASK 6
CAREER SUCCESS MAP QUESTIONNAIRE (CSMQ)

Take the CSMQ at the end of this chapter; it should only take 5 to 10 minutes. Don't agonize over the choices for each of the 30 items. Just answer candidly to the best of your ability.

Have you taken the CSMQ? If not, do not pass Go. Do not collect your $200. It is important to take it before reading the following interpretation of results. The CSMQ measures your preferences for five types of career orientations. This is not a career interest survey because it does not explore your interests in specific occupations. Instead, it assesses your orientation in the following broad career categories:

CAREER ORIENTATION	ORIENTATION CHARACTERISTICS
Advancement	Quest for the top of the organizational hierarchy and status system; focus on upward mobility, status, and power
Security	Sense of belonging, long-term employment, and being valued; focus on job security and sincere recognition
Freedom	Control over work processes and creative freedom; focus on minimal supervision, independence, less structure
Balance	Meaningful balance between work, important relationships, and personal development; focus on flexibility and efficiency
Challenge	Desire for excitement, "cutting-edge" opportunities, and adventure; focus on challenging projects, passionate causes

Now look at your scores from the CSMQ and make note of two things. First, identify your strongest orientation. If it is 9 or above, and your next highest score is 7 or less, then you have a dominant career orientation. Dr. Derr points out that not all individuals have dominant career orientations. He explains that this may be because they have insufficient work and/or life experience to have discovered their preferred orientation. Another explanation is that some individuals are in a career or life transition and are unsure of their career orientation.[3] So don't think that you did something wrong if your scores for the

---

[3] Derr, C. B. (1994). *Managing the new careerists: The diverse career success orientations of today's workers.* San Francisco: Jossey-Bass.

five categories are bunched together in the 4 to 8 range. The second point of interest is to look at your two highest scoring categories. If they are within a point of each other and have strong intensity levels (9 or above), then you should examine the connections between the two orientations. For example, if you scored a 10 on Challenge and a 9 on Advancement, that suggests to me that your career aspirations will be best met by joining a medium to large corporation that is considered an exciting place to work, or that is the industry leader in innovative products and services. These connections are especially important if there is a wide gap between the scores of your two highest categories and the remaining three categories.

Keep in mind that the purpose of career assessment tools is to improve your awareness of self and to suggest potentially suitable careers that fit your unique profile. They do not guarantee success nor do they mandate your pursuit of a specified path. Use them to illuminate your own understanding of who you are and what you can contribute to a particular occupation. If you have had a dream job or company in mind for some time now, I urge you to research that opportunity. Remember that career aspirations and dreams are much more heart and gut than they are mental exercises.

VALUES

The second key component of learning who you are is a thorough recognition of your core values. Careful reflection and understanding of personal values is increasingly important for career success. Part of that importance is that you want to ensure that your most fundamental personal values are embraced by your organization, or at the very least, are not in direct conflict with those of your organization. As organizational core values have taken on a heightened role in recent years, you are not likely to last long in a company where your values are not aligned. In fact, companies with strong corporate cultures tend to rigorously hire new employees based on the fit between employee and organizational values. Dr. Barbara Moses identifies a couple of other compelling reasons to clarify our personal and work-related values.

> Why do *you* work? Our values play a crucial role in determining how we feel about ourselves and our work. Increasingly, people are questioning their values in light of the frantic pace of their lives . . . we may discover that what we *think* is important and what really *is* important to us are two very different things. Staying in touch with our values can help us avoid making mistakes in managing our careers.[4]

Congruence between our actions and our values affects the feelings we have about our jobs, companies, and overall career satisfaction. Another important reason to focus on values is to make better decisions in the management of our careers. Be extremely cautious about accepting offers with companies or in

---

[4] Moses, B. (1997). *Career intelligence: The 12 new rules for work and life success.* San Francisco: Berrett-Koehler Publishers, p. 151.

industries where your most cherished personal values are likely to be compromised, values such as integrity, religious beliefs, or individuality as examples.

 TREK TASK 7
PERSONAL MISSION AND VALUES

Go to the FranklinCovey Web site at www.franklincovey.com and click on the "Library & Resources" tab. Then click on the "Mission Statement Builder" link. Complete the free mission statement development exercise. It will help you create a personal mission statement and identify your most important personal values.

Beyond personal values are numerous work-related values that need to be recognized. To help you identify those work-related values that are most important to you, please complete the job descriptions exercise on pages 36–38 of this chapter.[5]

After you have identified the three values pertaining to your chosen job descriptions, please write them down. You may also want to write down an additional three to five personal or work-related values that are also important to your future career choices.

ENVIRONMENT

When considering career choices, especially those involving a change of employer, you need to understand what work environments you prefer. Toward the end of my doctoral program, when considering which universities to apply to for faculty positions, I focused mostly on business schools that offered a good balance of teaching and research. It was also my preference to go to an environment that was small but with good growth potential. I wanted to help shape programs and make a significant difference. A healthy quality of life for my family was also an important consideration. Not every business school could satisfy these requirements.

Consider the following questions about your preferred work environments.

- *Geographical.* Work in your current city? Your current region? United States? International?
- *Work setting.* Indoor office? Home? Car? Outdoors?
- *Work partners.* Work alone? Work with a small team (three or four)? Work with large teams?
- *Work focus.* People? Things? Data? Ideas?
- *Work surroundings.* Busy? Quiet? Interaction with coworkers? Interaction with customers?

---

[5] Exercise adapted from Sukiennik, D., Bendat, W., & Raufman, L. (2007). *The career fitness program: Exercising your options,* 8th ed. Upper Saddle River, NJ: Prentice Hall, pp. 63–64.

- *Stress level.* E.R. is calm? Flexible deadlines? Structured and routine tasks?
- *Company size.* Small? Medium? Large?
- *Company age.* Start-up? Moderate growth? Explosive growth? Maturity? Decline?
- *Preferences.* Favorite industry? Favorite companies?

Answers to these questions will help refine what you are looking for in terms of incentives provided by the job. It's not that you always want to be in your favorite comfort zone, because you will want to be stretched from time to time. However, you want to be in an environment that gives you the best chance for exceptional performance results and satisfies your most critical motives. Nor is it likely that you will find a work environment that satisfies all of your preferences. You need to determine which of those preferences are absolutely essential to you, and which are "nice to have" features in a given work environment.

PERSONALITY

Your unique personality traits can have a major impact on your effectiveness in work roles. If you recall, Holland's research posits that personality is the key variable to consider for making effective career choices. Keep in mind that personality traits tend to be more stable over time than your skills, and therefore, they are less easily changed by either you or a boss. Research has shown that certain personality types do better in specific occupations. For example, people high in extroversion perform better in sales positions. Perhaps the most widely used of all personality instruments is the Myers-Briggs Type Indicator (or MBTI). The result of your candid responses to the MBTI items is a four-letter code that suggest a personality profile based upon four dimensions.

I will tell you as a means of information and self-disclosure that my four-letter type is ENFJ, and ENFJs tend to have the following characteristics: good group leaders, charismatic, value cooperation, nurturing and supportive, sometimes idealize relationships, effective communicators, empathize well with others, tend to be restless, and like things organized. Some occupations suggested by this personality type are

- Ministers
- Charismatic teachers
- Media, stage, and screen actors
- Executives

There is additional interpretation and for me, it is right on the money. I don't claim that your results will fit your self-perception as closely as mine do, but the MBTI results will enlighten you and perhaps raise a few questions and potential career paths as well. If you do not have access to the MBTI at either your educational institution or place of employment, then here is another alternative for you to pursue (and it's free).

TREK TASK 8

ONLINE PERSONALITY ASSESSMENT

Go to the *Princeton Review* Web site (www.princetonreview.com/cte/). On the Career page, click on the "Find Your Path with Career Quiz" link and complete this quiz. You will then receive two color types as output along with an interpretation about occupations and work environments that fit you best. Print the output page.

Do you feel like you know yourself better now? I purposefully chose to explore your motives and aspirations before looking at your skills. In my experience, skills are less predictive of career fulfillment and satisfaction. But job requirements are usually developed with skills in mind, not aspirations and motives. To analyze your fit with a prospective job opportunity you must know your skills. In mountaineering terms, you must know what you brought in your pack (and just as important, what you don't have in your pack), and the equipment you have at your disposal.

TREK LIST

☐ **CAREER ASPIRATIONS.**   I have identified a dream job, company, or industry and took the Career Success Map Questionnaire to understand my dominant career orientations.

☐ **PERSONAL VALUES.**   I understand the importance of aligning personal values with organizational values; I feel confident that I know what personal values I cherish the most.

☐ **WORK ENVIRONMENT PREFERENCES.**   Do I have any strong preferences for particular work environments that I believe allow me to perform at my highest levels?

☐ **PERSONALITY TRAITS.**   I have taken some type of personality test to increase my self-awareness and to learn of potentially suitable occupations given my unique personality profile.

 TREK TASK

JOB DESCRIPTIONS EXERCISE

From the 15 possible job descriptions below, circle the *three* you find most appealing as career possibilities. The value implied by each job description and examples of job titles that emphasize each value are provided on page 38 . . . so don't peek until after you choose your three favorite descriptions.

1. An opportunity to help people in a personal way. Meet and deal with the public in a meaningful relationship. Help to make

the world a better place to live. Pay and benefits in accordance with experience.

2. Do your own thing! Work with abstract ideas. Develop new ideas and things. Nonroutine. A chance to work on your own or as a member of a creative team. Flexible working conditions.

3. A professional position. Position of responsibility. Secretarial assistance provided. Pay dependent on experience and initiative. Position requires a high level of education and training. Job benefits are high pay and public recognition.

4. A job with a guaranteed annual salary in a permanent position with a secure, stable company. No employee layoffs in the company's 30-year history. Union representation for nonexecutive positions. Position guarantees annual cost-of-living pay increases. Excellent retirement benefits.

5. Looking for an interesting job? One that requires research, thinking, and problem solving? Do you like to deal with theoretical concepts? This job demands constant updating of information and ability to deal with new ideas. An opportunity to work with creative and intellectually stimulating people.

6. This job requires an extraordinary person. The job demands risk and daring. Ability to deal with exciting tasks. Excellent physical health a necessity. You must be willing to travel.

7. An ideal place to work. An opportunity to work with people you really like and—just as important—who really like you. A friendly, congenial atmosphere. Get to know your coworkers as friends. Pay and benefits dependent on training and/or experience.

8. Work in a young, fast-growing company. Great opportunities for advancement. Starting pay is low, but rapid promotion is possible. Many opportunities and directions for further advancement. Your only limitations are your own energy and initiative. Pay and benefits related to level of responsibility.

9. Set your own pace! Set your own working conditions. Flexible hours. Choose your own team or work alone. Salary based on your own initiative and time on the job.

10. Start at the bottom and work your way up. You can become president of the firm. You should have the ability to learn while you work. Quality and productivity will be rewarded by rapid advancement and recognition for a job well done. Salary contingent on rate of advancement.

11. Ability to direct work tasks of others in a variety of activities. Leadership qualities in controlling workforce and maintaining

production schedules. Coordinate work of large management team. Evaluate work completed. Hiring and firing
responsibilities.

12. Great opportunity for money! High salary, elaborate expense
    accounts, stock options, extra pay for extra work. Christmas
    bonus. All fringe benefits paid by company. High pay for the
    work you do.

13. Are you tired of a dull, routine job? Try your hand at many
    tasks, meet new people, work in different situations and set-
    tings. Be a jack-of-all-trades.

14. Does the thought of a desk job turn you off? This job is for the
    active person who enjoys using energy and physical abilities
    because it requires brisk and lively movement.

15. Opportunity to express your personal convictions in all phases
    of your job. Devote your lifestyle to your work.

JOB DESCRIPTIONS INTERPRETATION

JOB NUMBER	VALUE	EXAMPLES OF JOB TITLES EMPHASIZING VALUE
1	Helping others	Social worker, counselor, teacher
2	Creativity	Writer, artist, graphic designer
3	Prestige	Executive, politician, doctor
4	Security	Educational administrator, executive assistant, mechanic
5	Intellect	Researcher, mathematician, scientist
6	Adventure	FBI, CIA investigator, firefighter, archaeologist, military
7	Association	Educator, restaurant worker, tour guide, public relations
8	Advancement	Assistant sales manager, engineer, professional services firms
9	Independence	Landscaper, contract IT worker, marketing rep
10	Productivity	Sales rep, clerk, bookkeeper
11	Power	Manager, team leader, company president
12	Money	Stockbroker, accountant, real estate developer, technology executive
13	Variety	Electrician, plumber, lawyer, freelance editor
14	Physical activity	Personal trainer, P.E. teacher, parks and recreation services worker
15	Lifestyle	Minister, guidance counselor, consultant

CAREER SUCCESS MAP QUESTIONNAIRE (CSMQ)

Copyright © 2005, Novations Group, Inc.

Basic talents, values, and motives have an impact when decisions are made about careers. The following survey is designed to help you understand your career orientation. You can't fail this test; there are no right or wrong answers.

Each item contains two statements. Choose the one you feel most accurately describes you or is more true of you. You must choose one of the statements, even though you may not like either or you may like both of them. Do not skip any pair of statements or circle both alternatives in one set. Circle the letter to the left of the one sentence you select as the most reflective of you. Do not spend a lot of time weighing your answers.

Circle one letter in each pair.

1. (V) I like to organize myself and others to win.
   (X) I like to do my own thing in an organization.

2. (Y) Work must be balanced by time for leisure and the development of significant relationships.
   (V) Personal needs must be subordinated for me to get ahead.

3. (W) I would like to work in an organization which rewards hard work, loyalty, and dedication.
   (X) I like setting my own goals and accomplishing them at my own pace and in my own way.

4. (V) I am aggressive and have good analytical and people skills.
   (Y) I am able to keep a good perspective between the needs of my work and the needs of my family.

5. (X) I want to work independently.
   (W) I like being a company person.

6. (Z) I enjoy working as a consultant or "trouble shooter" and getting turned on by an exciting project.
   (V) I enjoy working in a situation where I am the leader and am responsible for achieving certain objectives.

7. (Y) My relationships outside of work are as important to me as my career.
   (Z) My relationships outside of work take a back seat to my work when I am in the middle of a very exciting project.

8. (X) The most important thing to me is freedom.
   (Y) The most important thing to me is maintaining work/life perspective.

9. (W) I am competent, loyal, trustworthy, and hard-working.
   (V) I am politically skillful, a good leader, and a good administrator.

I can be described as:

10. (X) Self-reliant.
    (Y) Balanced.

11. (Z) One who gets "turned on" by exciting projects.
    (X) One who likes to be his/her own boss.

12. (Y) In equilibrium but divided.
    (Z) Adventurous and competitive.

13. (X) Self-reliant, self-sufficient.
    (Z) Imaginative, enthused.

14. (W) Stable and tenacious.
    (X) Independent and self-directed.

15. (V) One who plans and organizes extremely well.
    (Z) One who analyzes situations and develops creative, new solutions.

16. (Z) An expert in my field.
    (W) A solid citizen.

17. (W) Able to modify my own goals to accommodate organizational goals and leaders.
    (Y) Intent on finding a way to make the organization's goals and my personal goals converge.

A personal goal is to:

18. (X) Control my own destiny.
    (Y) Not let work interfere with the needs of my personal life.

It is important to:

19. (W) Have a job where there is security and a sense of belonging.
    (Y) Be able to devote time to family and other personal activities.

I prefer:

20. (V) A career with potential for promotions.
    (Z) The opportunity to tackle challenging problems or tasks.

21. (V) I like being at the center of influence.
    (W) I value long-term employment, acceptance, and being valued by the organization.

22. (V) I view knowing the right people and making the right friends as important to career advancement.
    (X) I view being able to develop my career along my own areas of interest as the critical factor.

23. (Y) The bottom line for me is gaining a sense of balance between work and private life.
    (W) The bottom line for me is stability, appreciation, and having a secure place in the organization.

24. (X) I would like a position with maximum self-control and autonomy.
    (V) I would like to be in the inner circle.

25. (W) The bottom line for me is stability, appreciation, and having a secure place in the organization.
    (V) The bottom line for me is advancing up the organization.

26. (V) I view financial success and increased power and prestige as important measures of career success.
    (Y) I view success in my career as having equal time for work, family, and self-development.

I would rather:

27. (Z) Excel in my field.
    (W) Be considered dependable and loyal.

I prefer:

28. (W) Working with a team on a long-term and steady basis.
    (Z) Working with a task force or project group on a fast-paced and short-term basis.

29. (Z) Professional development and continued training are important for their own sake.
    (X) Professional development is important as a means to an end of becoming an expert and gaining more flexibility and independence.

30. (Y) The bottom line for me is to seek an equilibrium between personal and professional life.
    (Z) The bottom line for me is excitement and stimulation.

SCORING

Once you have completed the test, go back through it and add up the number of times you circled the letter "V." Then do the same with each of the other letters, writing the number in the space provided below. If you have completed the test accurately up to this point, the grand total will be 30 (V + W + X + Y + Z = 30).

	Advancement	Security	Freedom	Balance	Challenge
Score	V = _____	W = _____	X = _____	Y = _____	Z = _____

Orientation Intensity Levels   Strong 9 – 12   Average 4 – 8   Weak 0 – 3

What Is in Your Pack?
Talents, Skills, and Traits

Everybody has talent, it's just a matter of moving around until you've discovered what it is.

—*George Lucas*

Confidence can get you where you want to go, and getting there is a daily process. It's so much easier when you feel good about yourself, your abilities and talents.

—*Donald Trump*

The new landscape of business careers is much less about titles and positions than about skills and unique contributions of value to an organization's activities. As we prepare to ascend the mountain, it is essential to have the right equipment in our packs. This chapter is designed to help you identify your strengths and weaknesses. We'll do an equipment check, both from the perspective of employers (what do they want you to have in your pack?) and from your own viewpoint (what skills do you actually have in your repertoire right now?). First, we need to make some distinctions between three terms that are sometimes used interchangeably, but that really are different—talents, skills, and traits.

TALENTS, SKILLS, AND TRAITS

Talents

You have unique talents! Although you may not have thought yourself to be very talented, you do have some special abilities. Based on a landmark research effort by the Gallup organization, the world's greatest managers define talent as "a recurring pattern of thought, feeling, or behavior that can be productively applied."[1] It is like a unique filter that each of us has and it influences how we process information, what information is processed, and how we react to our environmental circumstances. The key to exceptional performance, according to Buckingham and Coffman (authors of the Gallup findings), "is finding the match between your talents and your role."[2] Keep in mind that you are not likely to discover all of your talents at once. Life reveals to us over time additional talents previously hidden from our consciousness. As we develop our talents, we often identify new talents.

How do talents differ from skills and from traits? One distinction is that skills can be more easily taught (and learned) than either talents or traits. "Skills are the how-to's of a role. They are capabilities that can be transferred from one person to another."[3] Let's illustrate the distinction with accountants. Accountants use skills in mathematics and operating software applications such as QuickBooks to successfully do their jobs. Now read about a specific talent of the best accountants related by Buckingham and Coffman:

> Through Gallup's studies of great accountants, we have discovered that one of their most important talents is an innate love of precision. Ask a great accountant—not any accountant, but a great accountant—when he smiles and he will tell you, "When the books balance." When the books balance, his world is perfect . . . if you think about it, for the person blessed with an innate love of precision, accountancy must be a wonderful job. Every time his books balance he experiences absolute perfection in his work. How many of us can claim that? A love of precision is not a skill. Nor is it knowledge. It is a talent. If you don't possess it, you will never excel as an accountant. If someone does not have this talent as part of his filter, there is very little a manager can do to inject it.[4]

John Wooden, the renowned former UCLA basketball coach, once said this about talent:

> There may be a hundred great coaches of whom you have never heard in basketball, football, or any sport who will probably never receive the acclaim they deserve simply because they have not been blessed with the talent. Although not every coach can win consistently with talent, no coach can win without it.[5]

"The Coach" was referring to the talent of players on his team, not the coach's talent (and he had considerable talent himself). Talent is essential to world-class performance levels but hard to convey on a résumé and also difficult for interviewers to discover in a 30-minute interview. At the very least, you need to start identifying your best talents. From Gallup's extensive research with more than 80,000 managers, Buckingham and Coffman identified and categorized numerous talents. Each of their three categories will now be described along with the specific talents comprising that category.[6]

---

[1] Buckingham, M., & Coffman, C. (1999). *First, break all the rules: What the world's greatest managers do differently.* New York: Simon & Schuster, p. 71.

[2] Ibid., p. 71.

[3] Ibid., p. 83.

[4] Ibid., pp. 84–85.

[5] Ibid., p. 105.

[6] Ibid., pp. 85, 251–252.

Striving Talents

These talents relate to the inner drives and motivations of a person; they are what makes the person tick (what gets you out of bed every morning).

- ☐ **Achiever**   A drive that is internal, constant, and self-imposed
- ☐ **Kinesthetic**   A need to expend physical energy
- ☐ **Stamina**   Capacity for physical endurance
- ☐ **Competition**   A need to gauge your success comparatively
- ☐ **Desire**   A need to claim significance through independence, excellence, risk, and recognition
- ☐ **Competence**   A need for expertise or mastery
- ☐ **Belief**   A need to orient your life around certain prevailing values
- ☐ **Mission**   A drive to put your beliefs in action
- ☐ **Service**   A drive to be of service to others
- ☐ **Ethics**   A clear understanding of right and wrong guiding your actions
- ☐ **Vision**   A drive to paint value-based word pictures about the future

Thinking Talents

These talents relate to how a person thinks, processes information, and structures daily activities.

- ☐ **Focus**   An ability to set goals and to use them every day to guide actions
- ☐ **Discipline**   A need to impose structure onto life and work
- ☐ **Arranger**   An ability to orchestrate
- ☐ **Work Orientation**   A need to mentally rehearse and review
- ☐ **Gestalt**   A need to see order and accuracy
- ☐ **Responsibility**   A need to assume personal accountability for your work
- ☐ **Concept**   An ability to develop a framework by which to make sense of things
- ☐ **Performance Orientation**   A need to be objective and to measure performance
- ☐ **Strategic Thinking**   An ability to play out alternative scenarios in the future
- ☐ **Business Thinking**   The financial application of the strategic thinking talent
- ☐ **Problem Solving**   An ability to think things through with incomplete data
- ☐ **Formulation**   An ability to find coherent patterns within incoherent data sets
- ☐ **Numerical**   An affinity for numbers
- ☐ **Creativity**   An ability to break existing configurations in favor of more effective/appealing ones

Relating Talents

This final category of talents relates to a person's interactions and relationships with others, whether strangers or friends and family.

☐ **Woo**	A need to gain the approval of others
☐ **Empathy**	An ability to identify the feelings and perspectives of others
☐ **Relator**	A need to build bonds that last
☐ **Multirelator**	An ability to build an extensive network of acquaintances
☐ **Interpersonal**	An ability to purposely capitalize upon relationships
☐ **Individualized Perception**	An awareness of and attentiveness to individual differences
☐ **Developer**	A need to invest in others, deriving satisfaction in so doing
☐ **Stimulator**	An ability to create enthusiasm and drama
☐ **Team**	A need to build feelings of mutual support
☐ **Positivity**	A need to look on the bright side
☐ **Persuasion**	An ability to persuade others logically
☐ **Command**	An ability to take charge
☐ **Activator**	An impatience to move others to action
☐ **Courage**	An ability to use emotion to overcome resistance

 TREK TASK 9
YOUR BEST TALENTS

You've read through the list. Now review the talents in each of the three categories and place a checkmark next to each one that you honestly perceive as one of your talents. After doing that, go back through and circle only your best talents, those that really distinguish you from your peer group or that others often mention in glowing terms about you.

Skills

According to Bolles, "Your transferable skills are the most basic unit—the atoms—of whatever career you may choose."[7] There are actually two main types of skills—job-specific and transferable. *Job-specific skills* are those skills that are relevant to a particular job but not easily applied in other positions or occupations. Examples of such skills are operating a forklift, modeling

---

[7] Bolles, R. N. (2005). *What color is your parachute?* Berkeley, CA: Ten Speed Press, p. 138.

structural equations, or drawing blood from a person's finger. *Transferable skills* are typically broader in nature and are represented by action verbs, and they can be used in many different occupational settings. You need to understand very, *very* well exactly what skills you bring to the table. There are so many possible skills that I will not provide a list of choices here, but I won't leave you without any guidance on how to identify your best transferable skills. First, transferable skills are usually divided into three categories that should sound familiar to you from Chapter 3—skills related to processing *Data,* skills related to interacting with *People,* and skills related to working with *Things.* So write down action verbs that describe skills in each of these three areas. Second, remember the three types of skills from the Person–Job Fit model in Chapter 1—technical/functional, interpersonal, and problem-solving. Finally, if you are still struggling, the SAR process at the end of this chapter should assist you in identifying some important transferable skills.

Traits

Traits are more stable than skills and they are sometimes talked about in the same breath as personality characteristics. Think of them as the adjectives that describe how you use your skills. The following checklist gives you many choices of common traits. Put a check next to those that accurately describe you. A good way to identify your strongest traits is to think about how others describe your contribution at work or in student teams.

☐ Accurate	☐ Energetic	☐ Persevering
☐ Adaptable	☐ Enthusiastic	☐ Persistent
☐ Adventuresome	☐ Fair	☐ Practical
☐ Assertive	☐ Firm	☐ Professional
☐ Calm	☐ Flexible	☐ Punctual
☐ Cautious	☐ Honest	☐ Quick
☐ Charismatic	☐ Humane	☐ Rational
☐ Compassionate	☐ Humble	☐ Realistic
☐ Competent	☐ Impulsive	☐ Resourceful
☐ Consistent	☐ Independent	☐ Responsible
☐ Cooperative	☐ Innovative	☐ Self-motivated
☐ Courageous	☐ Intelligent	☐ Self-reliant
☐ Creative	☐ Knowledgeable	☐ Sensitive
☐ Decisive	☐ Loyal	☐ Sophisticated
☐ Deliberate	☐ Methodical	☐ Supportive
☐ Dependable	☐ Objective	☐ Tactful
☐ Diligent	☐ Open-minded	☐ Thorough
☐ Diplomatic	☐ Outgoing	☐ Unique
☐ Discreet	☐ Patient	☐ Versatile
☐ Dynamic	☐ Perceptive	☐ Vigorous

WHAT EQUIPMENT DO EMPLOYERS WANT YOU TO CARRY?

While it will not and should not drive your skill development, you need to at least be aware of the skills and traits that employers are seeking from applicants. Of course, individual job descriptions typically articulate specific requirements, but I will offer you two "wish" lists from diverse sources, along with a little personal commentary.

Survey Says

In a recent survey, employers ranked the following as the 10 most desired personal skills and qualities they are seeking in job candidates:[8]

1. Communication skills
2. Honesty/integrity
3. Interpersonal skills
4. Strong work ethic
5. Teamwork skills
6. Analytical skills
7. Motivation/initiative
8. Flexibility/adaptability
9. Computer skills
10. Detail-oriented

As you can see, this list consists of five skill sets and five traits. I don't find it surprising in our post-Enron business world that employers placed integrity as their most desired trait. Let me stress this again, and if you get nothing else from this book, get this: *Your personal integrity is everything! Never lie on a résumé.* Never perform unethically in a company to expand your personal wealth. You can't cheat your way to the top of the mountain!

Look at the three highest skill sets mentioned in the survey. Communication, interpersonal, and teamwork—they all relate to how well we interact with people. Business schools got the message about 15 years ago to focus on teamwork skills. We've heard the message for many years now about communication and interpersonal skills but have been slow to incorporate those into the curriculum. Pepper de Callier, former partner with the executive search firm Heidrick & Struggles, told our students about a conversation he had with the CEO of a medium-sized company. "The thing that is really lacking from the college graduates we've hired recently is they don't know how to write business letters." It's sadly true in many cases. We have become a rather lazy nation in terms of our communication skills. Despite the amount of writing required of

---

[8] National Association of Colleges and Employers. (2005). Job outlook 2005.

students in their courses, it still amazes me how many upper-level college students struggle to write competently. Don't procrastinate learning to communicate.

New American Professional

Tom Peters identified five characteristics of what he termed the "New American Professional."[9] They are different in their focus than the employers' top 10 list, but they are no less valuable to consider. How many of the five do you have right now?

1. At least one Distinctive (Towering) Competence
2. Projects-Is-Life Mentality
3. Client-service Obsessed
4. Networker Extraordinaire
5. Self-Reliant in Career Management (Me, Inc.)

So you have to be *really* good at something, skilled at managing and performing on projects, obsessed with knowing who your key clients are and with exceeding their expectations, an exceptional networking guru, and in command of forging your career. This book should help you with the fifth characteristic. The first characteristic takes some time to hone. So you will need to focus on the middle three characteristics. Piece of cake, right?

WHAT EQUIPMENT DO YOU HAVE?

There are several ways to discover your best skills. You can do skills self-assessments, take aptitude tests, and ask a spouse or other close friend who knows you well to articulate the skills they see you perform most effectively. Another, called the SAR approach (some experts refer to it as the STAR approach) is beneficial because it not only helps you identify prominent skills, but the process will greatly enhance your interviewing effectiveness.

SAR Stories

The SAR process is a powerful approach to showcase your best abilities and accomplishments. They are most effective when used to answer behavioral-based interview questions (e.g., Can you give me an example of how you have handled an irate customer? or Tell me about a time when you effectively led a team.). These short stories can also help you identify performance accomplishments to include on your résumé. The acronym SAR stands for Situation, Action, Result. Let's go over these three components in detail.

---

[9] Peters, T. (1999). *The circle of innovation: You can't shrink your way to greatness.* New York: Vintage, pp. 183–185.

Situation. As you think of a time when you demonstrated a particular talent, trait, or skill, you need to take a step back and clarify the situation in which it was used. What was the context of your actions? You don't need to provide every minute detail, only the most vital elements. What was the problem or opportunity facing you, your team, and/or your organization? How critical was the situation? What was your role or involvement? For example, was this situation part of your normal job responsibilities or something outside your routine tasks? Try to capture the critical elements of the situation in a couple of sentences. In most cases, the interviewer will be more concerned with the other two sections, the actions you took and the end result. If you were asked to describe how you behaved in a particular type of situation, make sure that you actually use a relevant situation.

Action. The centerpiece of the SAR story is what you did in the particular situation. What were *your* actions? Be careful when discussing team situations that you identify your individual contributions, not just what the team did. If you were asked to talk about a particular skill or trait, then you need to emphasize that unique item in your SAR story. Common skills and traits that you may be asked to illustrate are leadership, customer service, problem solving, closing a sale, conflict resolution, creativity, and integrity. The purpose of the SAR is to show your strengths in action and to give the interviewer a memorable (and true!) story to remember you compared with other applicants. So be specific in what skills or traits you used to address the situation you previously described. You may exhibit more than one skill or trait, and you may have to offer a brief rationale for your actions if it is not readily apparent.

Result. Like any good story, an expectation builds for a compelling ending. The result (or results) of your action needs to provide that strong finish. The most important element of the result is to offer a specific outcome, something that is tangible or measurable is the most effective. For example, "My calm resolution of the irate customer's issues led to him becoming a loyal customer and purchasing over $20,000 of merchandise in the past year." "The leadership that I provided to my senior project team resulted in the praise of the sponsoring organization, an A grade from our faculty advisor, and recognition as one of the three outstanding projects that semester." Keep in mind that the prospective employer wants to be assured that you will add value to the company, so emphasize organizational results where possible. There are some actions and situations that result in less easily measured outcomes. The effects of improving company morale and effective communication skills may be tougher to quantify, but you need to try anyway. Company awards and recognitions can also be good accomplishments to use here.

The SAR process is important because as you prepare a few of these you will refine the mental technique of packaging your achievements, skills, and best traits. When you are confronted by an interviewer's question for which you are ill-prepared, you can at least go through the SAR process in your mind and provide a specific experience that will leave a more positive impression with the interviewer. Key results that come out of your SAR stories can be conveyed on your résumé. The overall story you relate needs to be concise, keeping it under three minutes in most cases.

TREK TASK 10

SAR Practice

In the space below, write your own SAR story that demonstrates one of your best talents or skills identified previously in this chapter. Remember to briefly recap the specific situation, articulate the actions that you performed, and communicate the important results of those actions.

Situation:

Action(s):

Result(s):

Which of the three steps was the most challenging? How quantifiable were your results? You will not be able to prepare for every possible behavioral-based interview question, but if you understand the SAR process and are comfortable using it, your interview performance will increase significantly. In Chapter 10, we will further discuss interview preparation and I will provide you with a couple of example responses using the SAR technique. Okay, how is your oxygen level thus far? Let us recap.

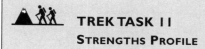

TREK TASK 11

Strengths Profile

In the chart that follows, please write your best talents, skills, and traits as identified throughout this chapter. This chart represents a profile of your individual strengths. Show the chart to at least one other person who knows you really well. Talk with that person about any differences in perception.

Review your Brand You statement that you created in Chapter 2. How consistent is your statement with this profile?

This concludes our most concentrated self-awareness portion of base camp, but keep an open mind about yourself as we proceed. The real work is just beginning. Next up—résumés, cover letters, and networking.

TALENTS	SKILLS	TRAITS
_____	_____	_____
_____	_____	_____
_____	_____	_____
_____	_____	_____
_____	_____	_____
_____	_____	_____
_____	_____	_____
_____	_____	_____
_____	_____	_____
_____	_____	_____

TREK LIST

☐ **TALENT SCOUT.**   I have identified my best striving, thinking, and relating talents; and I understand how talents, skills, and traits are distinct from one another.

☐ **SKILLS MIX.**   I have reflected on the skills that I have consistently demonstrated in past employment and educational experiences.

☐ **TRICK OR TRAITS.**   I have greater awareness of my best traits.

☐ **MARKETABLE QUALITIES.**   I know what employers are looking for and have considered the characteristics described by Tom Peters as the New American Professional.

☐ **SAR STORIES.**   I know how the SAR process works and I have practiced it with one of my strong skill areas.

☐ **OVERALL PROFILE.**   If an interviewer asks me about my strengths, I can talk meaningfully about two or three strengths with specific examples (SAR stories) that support my claims.

Your Passport
Résumé and Cover Letter

5

Enclosed is a ruff draft of my résumé.

Please disregard the attached résumé—it is terribly out of date.

If this resume doesn't blow your hat off, then please return it in the enclosed envelope.

I am sicking and entry-level position.

Here are my qualifications for you to overlook.

I am relatively intelligent, obedient, and as loyal as a puppy.

Note: Keep this résumé on top of the stack. Use all the others to heat your house.

I'll need $30K to start, full medical, three weeks vacation, stock options and ideally a European sedan.

Although I am seeking an accounting job, the fact that I have no actual experience in accounting may seem discouraging. However. . .

I'll starve without a job but don't feel you have to give me one.

Thank you for your consideration. Hope to hear from you shorty!

> — *actual cover letter quotes from* www.usewisdom.com/fun/

Before aspiring climbers can even get to base camp on Mount Everest, they have to pay a pretty steep financial price to obtain the proper passport and a permit to be on the mountain. Your permit for our trek has already been purchased (by acquiring this book). But your passport to Mount Career is a different matter. Your career passport is your written documentation that says who you are, professionally speaking. There are two documents that you need to learn to complete perfectly (flawlessly may be a better word)—the résumé and the cover letter. Of the two documents, the résumé is the most important, but don't ignore the value of a well-written cover letter. Base camp has concentrated thus far on learning about yourself, but you still have to package yourself in an effective way on paper.

This chapter provides you with examples and guidelines to create and develop an effective résumé and cover letter. *How do you know if your passport is working on Mount Career? You obtain job interviews! That is the only purpose of these two documents.*

RÉSUMÉS

Read the following definition by Michael Bryant very carefully. It is both instructive and a bit scary.

> Resume: An ingenious device that turns a human being into an object (an eight and a half by eleven inches piece of paper). This transformation device is then often used to try and convince people we have never met to invest thousands of dollars in us, by hiring us for a job we have not yet specifically identified.[1]

Your mission as you develop your résumé, should you choose to accept it, is to make it persuasive enough to prospective employers that they invite you for an interview. It has to convince them that you have enough potential to do the job and contribute to their organizations and that it merits at least 30 minutes of their time to conduct an initial interview with you. Keep in mind as you work through this tedious process that when it comes to résumés, beauty is in the eye of the beholder. If you ask multiple individuals to critique your résumé, you are very likely to get some mixed messages about format and wording choices. While there is no universally accepted "perfect" résumé, there are some generally accepted guidelines for professional résumés.

Types of Résumé

Despite the lack of a universal standard for résumé format, there are two widely used types of résumés—chronological and functional. Other lesser used types are the achievement résumé and various hybrids of the chronological and functional résumés. We will stick to the two major résumé types, explaining the differences in format and the pros and cons of each of these two approaches.

Chronological. The most commonly used format is the chronological résumé, so named because it provides a time-based, or chronological, review of your career. You list your current (or most recent) educational and employment situation, and then the résumé proceeds in reverse chronological order. Dates are provided for degree completions in the Education section, and for employment tenures in the Employment History section. Two main advantages to this format are

- *Ease of creation.* This is the easiest way to create a résumé for the first time, or to convey your work history at any point in your career.
- *Shows career progression.* Works best if you have no significant gaps in your employment and you are applying for the next position in an occupational path (e.g., your current job is marketing manager and you are applying for V.P. of marketing).

---

[1] Quoted in Bolles, R. N. (2001). *What color is your parachute?* Berkeley, CA: Ten Speed Press, p. 21.

The two primary disadvantages are

- *Gaps can be a red flag.* Related to the last advantage, lengthy breaks in your employment history can be a point of concern for employers. In this era of layoffs and greater career turbulence, it is less of an issue but still be prepared to explain any prolonged gaps (especially if you are currently unemployed).
- *Emphasizes positions more than skills.* If you are applying for a position or industry for which you have minimal work experience, this is easier for employers to spot with a chronological résumé.

Three examples of the chronological résumé are shown at the end of the chapter.

Functional. A functional résumé emphasizes personal competencies gained from the combination of your educational and employment experiences. It is particularly effective in the two situations mentioned as problematic for chronological résumés—gaps in work history and lack of direct experience. The major plus with the functional résumé is that your transferable skills are easily identified by readers of the résumé. It can show clusters of skills that you have acquired in different settings, functional skills such as customer service, managing people, financial analysis, problem solving, and so forth. These skills areas become your main headings below which you bullet-point key results and more specific skills within those broad functional areas.

Résumé Guidelines

To follow are several commonly agreed-upon components for effective résumés, along with some personal comments about each of those components. Specific guidelines for completing each component are also offered.

RÉSUMÉ COMPONENT	SUGGESTIONS/COMMENTS
Name	Important to make your name stand out, although that depends on the type of position and level of competition for the position. Use bold font and make the font size somewhat larger than the rest of the document (nothing above 18-point font though); all caps helps, too. Do not include your full middle name, if you have one. Middle initials are appropriate.
Contact information	Make sure it is accurate and that you offer appropriate telephone numbers (for example, you may not want a prospective employer to call your current office phone). E-mail addresses should be included, but be careful with any "cute" or unprofessional addresses that you may be using: Remember that everything you include on this document conveys something about you.
Objective	Should be the first component in the body of your résumé. The more precise and tailored to the position the better. At the very least, you should specify the type of position; mentioning the industry helps even more.

(Continued)

Education	Details current degree program and any Associate degrees. List them in reverse chronological order (current program first). Bold the degree, and make sure you know the degree you are earning. Indicate your expected graduation date. Other items that can be included in this section include program major, minor, or emphasis areas; GPA (if at least 3.0); relevant coursework (don't list every course you have taken); and any important educational achievements, such as the dean's list, unique projects or programs, and scholarships.
Work experience	Should come before the Education section if your experience is relevant to the sought-after position. List current (or most recent) job first and then proceed in reverse chronological order. You must identify the position, company name and location (city and state are sufficient), and dates of employment. For each position, describe important skills used and accomplishments. Never mention the reasons for leaving a position. How far back should you go? Usually three to four jobs or 10 to 12 years is sufficient for detailed descriptions.
Skills and qualifications	This section can come anywhere after the Objective section. Include technical skills, people skills, functional expertise, and any other professional skills and accomplishments that you want to bring to the reader's attention. Be careful to not include too many skills or traits: This will make the employer skeptical.
References	Not necessary for the résumé; at most, put a statement at the bottom that says "References are available upon request." Employers assume that you have professional references and can provide them at a future time.
Overall length	One page is the standard for new college graduates; two pages are acceptable if you have significant work experience. If it is less than three-fourths of one page it will look too brief, but longer than two pages is too long.
No *I* in résumé	Don't use the pronoun *I* to describe your experience or qualifications.
Flawless grammar	One blatant spelling error or grammatical mistake is usually sufficient ground to remove your résumé from further consideration.

Beyond these specific guidelines for the common elements of a professional résumé, there are a few fundamental principles you need to consider as you refine this document.

- Be accurate in both factual content and spelling: *It is never appropriate to fabricate items on your résumé.*
- Tailor your résumé to the specific opening for which you are applying.
- Lead with your strengths relative to the job requirements. Remember that the average résumé will be initially examined for only 15 to 60 seconds depending on who you ask, so your best selling points need to be first and foremost on your résumé.

- Emphasize results/accomplishments and skills more than duties and responsibilities.
- Give your résumé the "look and feel" test. Is the format visually appealing while remaining professional? Are the dates, fonts, and spacing all consistent throughout the résumé? Did I use a laser-quality printer and bond or résumé-appropriate paper for my final résumé copies?

Your résumé must ooze professionalism, and its creation requires one of the most difficult tasks for most of us—bragging about our accomplishments. Get others whose business wisdom you respect to take a look at your résumé and give you a quick critique. ***Finally, as you proceed on your trek, update your résumé at least every six months.*** You have to keep your passport current!

 TREK TASK 12
RÉSUMÉ REFINEMENT

Now is your opportunity to practice! Using the guidelines in this chapter and the examples at the end of the chapter, create (or revise) your professional résumé for an actual position that interests you. Identify two people you know who have some expertise with résumés. Ask them to critique your résumé and provide candid feedback. Use their feedback to fine-tune your résumé.

COVER LETTERS

The second document that makes up your passport is the cover letter. With the advent of more electronically transmitted résumés, cover letters have taken a backseat to résumés in terms of importance (some companies don't ask you to e-mail a cover letter, only a résumé). *Do not ignore them.*

A few years ago a member of the HR department at Legoland came to my Careers class and shared a memorable experience about the value of a well-crafted and grammatically sound cover letter. He related that while hiring for a managerial position, the process came down to two final candidates. They had each interviewed with several key executives at Legoland California and the two were both deemed as very qualified for the position, and both candidates demonstrated a strong fit with the company's values. The two applicant files were pulled and reviewed one more time, just to see if anything might distinguish either candidate. Their cover letters were read carefully this time. As is often the case, the résumés received greater attention when the application was first received. One cover letter was flawlessly written, very professional, and with a positive tone. The second cover letter was written with an enthusiastic tone but contained numerous spelling and grammatical flaws. The candidate who wrote the first cover letter was offered (and accepted) the job. Every (and I mean *every*) point of contact you have with a prospective employer has the potential to either eliminate you from the running or catapult you to the top of the list so take the time needed to write a professional cover letter.

Objectives and Basic Format

The bottom line with the cover letter is to land you an interview, the same effectiveness indicator as the résumé. The cover letter has two other complementary purposes: (a) to capture the employer's interest and attention; and (b) to provide evidence of your fit with the company and/or the position.

The cover letter, like other business letters, has a heading section, the letter body, and then an ending section. The *heading* should provide your contact info, which can be done by either duplicating the résumé contact info on the cover letter, by placing your cover letter on company letterhead (if appropriate), or by simply typing in your address and phone number. The date comes next and then the name, title, and contact information of the intended recipient of your letter. Your *ending* section contains a courteous phrase such as "Sincerely," or "Respectfully," and after at least three blank lines, your name. *Make sure and sign your name*—forgetting to sign is a common mistake especially if you are sending out a mass mailing of résumés. You may also put the word "Enclosure" underneath your printed name to signify that you have enclosed another document—your résumé in this case.

It is in the *letter body* that cover letters differ from other types of business correspondence. The three main components of the cover letter will now be explained in detail.

Opening Paragraph. Prior to the paragraph, you must write your salutation. You should avoid sending a cover letter that opens with "To Whom It May Concern," if at all possible. This salutation shows a lack of effort in researching the name of the HR director, hiring manager, or some other specific person to whom your cover letter and résumé should be directed. If you know the person fairly well, you should use his or her first name. Otherwise, use Mr. or Ms. and the last name of the individual. It is not desirable to use the full name (e.g., "Dear Troy Nielson").

The opening paragraph should clearly introduce your reason for writing and give them a reason to be interested. Typically, opening paragraphs consist of only two to three sentences. There are three possible cover letter reasons:

1. *Advertised openings.* In this case you need to indicate that you have interest in the specific position that you found advertised in <name the specific source>.

2. *Network referrals.* If a member of your network told you about a position or simply referred you to send a résumé to a particular individual, then you need to indicate that in your opening sentence (e.g., "David Bennett, a great colleague of mine, suggested that I contact you about the Corporate Trainer position that just opened at your company.")

3. *No current openings.* You can use this type of letter when you really want to work for an organization but they don't appear to have any posted openings (either printed or on the Internet) for which you are qualified. Focus on your passion for the company and its needs.

Fit/Sales Pitch. Arguably the most important portion of the cover letter, the one or two middle paragraphs of your cover letter need to sell what you have to offer the organization and demonstrate a sufficient fit with the organization's needs and/or the job requirements. This is a good place to show that you have researched the organization. Focus on how you can help them meet their challenges and objectives. If two paragraphs are used, the first is typically to highlight your primary qualifications and skills. The second emphasizes the organization and its needs, describing how you fit with those needs. A more innovative approach advocated by career professionals in recent years is illustrated in the sample cover letter at the end of this chapter. Key job requirements and your qualifications that meet those requirements are laid out side by side in concise terms. This format immediately shows a prospective employer that (a) you meet the basic requirements and (b) that you care about the fit. The content of these paragraphs should not simply regurgitate what is on your résumé. Instead, your cover letter should motivate the reader to pay more attention to your résumé.

Closing Paragraph. There are two important guidelines for the closing paragraph. First, keep the ball in your court. Don't leave things completely in the hands of the prospective employer. Indicate that you will follow up to discuss an interview and give the employer a reasonable time frame (one week is typical). Then make sure that you *do* follow up if you have not yet heard from the company. Second, you want to leave a positive and grateful tone with the reader. Thank the person for the time and consideration given while reviewing your qualifications.

Two final points need to be made about cover letters. Don't overuse the word *I*. It comes across as too self-centered, especially if it comes at the beginning of most of the sentences in the letter. Unlike résumés though, it is appropriate to use *I* in the cover letter—just not in every sentence. Finally, remember the Legoland lesson—proofread and have others read your cover letter. It should be just as accurate and perfectly written as your résumé.

 TREK TASK 13

COVER LETTER CREATION

Practice creating a cover letter. Identify a specific job opening that interests you. Then, using the guidelines in this chapter and the example at the end of the chapter, create (or revise) your cover letter for that position. Ask one of your peers to review the letter, proofread it, and offer any suggestions for improvement.

So that is your passport—a professional résumé and cover letter. Work hard at refining these documents. Without this passport, you are not likely to go too far up Mount Career. There are two factors that lessen the importance of these two documents to your career success. One is your credibility that comes from a stellar performance track record and professional reputation. For example, do you think that if Bill Gates wanted a position at a startup technology company that the CEO would say, "Okay, Mr. Gates, send us a résumé and we'll consider your application"? Usually what happens is that once you develop a strong reputation in an industry or region, then other companies usually come courting you for positions, a very nice situation. The second factor that can reduce your reliance upon résumés and cover letters is to get more help from your traveling party—your professional network!

TREK LIST

☐ **RÉSUMÉ**   I have a professional résumé that adheres to principles of effective résumés; formatting is consistent and makes good use of white space; there are *zero* spelling errors; the content emphasizes my best accomplishments and skills.

☐ **COVER LETTER**   I know how to create a tailored one-page cover letter that expresses my interest in a position, my fit with company expectations, and my desire for an interview; this document also has *zero* spelling errors and is professional in both appearance and tone.

SAMPLE RÉSUMÉ

TROY R. NIELSON

123 COUGARS RULE DRIVE
HIGHLAND, UT 84003
WEB PAGE: www.uvsc.edu/profpages/nielsotr

HOME PHONE: (801) 121-2121
CELL PHONE: (801) 888-9999
E-MAIL: nielsotr@uvsc.edu

DIRECTOR/MANAGER OF TRAINING & DEVELOPMENT
Mentoring/Employee Development…Training Program Design and Implementation

SUMMARY OF QUALIFICATIONS

- Track record of high performance in business education/training/consulting for 11 years.
- Made 20 presentations on mentoring and human resource processes in the past five years.
- Provided pro bono organizational and employee development consulting services to business executives, healthcare professionals, and not-for-profit organizations.
- Developed innovative new courses (In the Executive's Chair, Career Development) that focus on practical applications and interaction with business executives.
- Over 15 years of leadership experience in professional, academic, and volunteer positions.
- Consummate team player with an entrepreneurial, creative mindset.
- Excellent written communication, interpersonal, and presentation skills.
- Speak, read, and write Portuguese.
- Proficient with Windows and Microsoft applications (Word, Excel, Access, PowerPoint).
- Working knowledge of WordPerfect, FrontPage, HTML, and Outlook.

WORK EXPERIENCE

California State University-San Marcos   San Marcos, CA   1998 – 2004
Associate Professor of Management and Organizational Behavior

Received research grants each year ($4000-5000) for the study of mentoring and human resource practices. Taught courses at the undergraduate level (organizational behavior, Inside the Executive's Chair, career development) and at the MBA level (management, human resource management). Served two years on the College of Business leadership group, two years as the Chair of the MBA Program Committee, and one year as Chair of the University Global Affairs Committee.
- Initiated and implemented an annual recognition program for business faculty and staff via an external partnership with the San Marcos Chamber of Commerce.
- Gained recognition at both national and regional conferences for outstanding research.
- Received the Outstanding Faculty Award for overall contributions in teaching, research, and service activities (1999-2000).
- Earn consistent student evaluations of 4.5+ (on a 5-point scale).
- Supervised over 20 senior team projects and 10 MBA projects (with 4 senior teams earning top project honors).

University of Utah   Salt Lake City, UT   1994 – 1998
Research Assistant and Teaching Instructor

Completed a field-based dissertation on mentoring effectiveness in a major healthcare organization. Conducted research related to organizational effectiveness and employee performance with faculty members. Taught courses in organizational behavior, interpersonal communication, and leadership.
- One of only two doctoral students in cohort to finish program in four years (others took 5+).
- Received two awards for teaching excellence (one from faculty and one from MBA students).
- Earned student evaluations that consistently exceeded department averages.

Andersen Consulting (now Accenture)	Phoenix, AZ	1991 – 1994
Senior Consultant		

Worked in the consumer products and healthcare industries as a programming team supervisor, functional analyst, and facilitator in the design and implementation of custom computer applications.
- Identified and corrected flaws in application modules; increased system accuracy by 20-50%.
- Promoted from Staff Consultant within two years of employment.
- Supervised a programming team to project completion on time and within budget.
- Served as primary liaison between technical design team and functional users on customer profitability project with a Fortune 1000 company.

EDUCATION

University of Utah	Salt Lake City, UT	1998
Ph.D. in Business Administration		
Emphasis in Organizational Behavior and Human Resource Management		

Brigham Young University	Provo, UT	1991
B.S. in Information Management		
Graduated Magna Cum Laude (GPA 3.83)		

SAMPLE RÉSUMÉ

NATHAN C. PEARSON

7032 Sequoia Court • Vista, California 92081
Home: (760) 757-7070 • Mobile: (760) 121-2121
e-mail: Pearson@csusm.edu

OBJECTIVE: To obtain an entry-level position in Marketing/Advertising

SUMMARY OF QUALIFICATIONS
- Four years of sales and administrative experience.
- Working knowledge of Microsoft Word, Excel, Access, PowerPoint, and SPSS.
- Personable and persuasive, team player, able to build rapport quickly.
- Good time management skills evidenced through work and academic schedules.
- Capable of dealing with a wide range of challenges and people.

EDUCATION
Bachelor of Science in Business Administration   December 2003
California State University San Marcos
Cumulative Grade Point Average: 3.0

WORK EXPERIENCE
Loan Net Inc.   Oceanside, CA   2002 – present
Administrative Assistant (Part Time)
- Handle large volumes of financial transactions, and maintain daily accounting records.
- Manage and train 2 new employees.
- Evaluate credit risk for new customers and collect overdue accounts receivable.

Bully's Surf Equipment   Oceanside, CA   1997 – 1998; 1999 – 2001
Production Operator (Part Time)
- Served on a production team to manufacture leashes, traction pads and board bags.
- Coordinated the distribution of products to domestic and international dealers.
- Gained experience in inventory management and organization.

Rancho Boardride Company   San Marcos, CA   1998 – 1999
Sales Associate (Part Time)
- Oversaw inventory purchasing, stocking, and mail order distribution to customers for sporting goods, clothing, and accessory dealer.
- Assisted with training of new employees.
- Managed cash registers; compiled transaction receipts and daily accounting information.

OTHER SKILLS/HONORS/ACTIVITIES
- Assisted in development of business plan for Livlocal.com (Internet start-up)
- Compiled comprehensive Marketing/Advertising campaign for Livlocal.com
- Surfing, traveling, painting and diverse musical interests

SAMPLE RÉSUMÉ

KARA DUGGINS

1007 INEEDAJOB AVENUE, UNIT #22 • ESCONDIDO, CA 92029
(760) 555-9999 • DUGGINS@CSUSM.EDU

OBJECTIVE

A public relations position in a fast growing company which includes the opportunity to travel.

SKILLS/STRENGTHS

- Highly motivated business professional with exceptional organizational skills and methodical approach to responsibilities; exemplary abilities in managing multiple demands simultaneously.
- Effective assessment and problem-solving skills; strong communication and editing skills.
- Ability to build positive, long-term relationships with clientele, co-workers, and all levels of management.

EDUCATION

Bachelor of Science in Business Administration

December 2002   California State University, San Marcos

- Service Sector Management Program, emphasis in developing relationships through networking, relationship management, and communication skills.
- Consulted for Seven-17 Restaurant & Bar as a Senior Experience project; developed an effective marketing plan that established brand recognition and increased the customer base for this new restaurant located in downtown San Diego.
- Have managed a full-time course schedule earning a 3.25 cumulative GPA while being totally self-supportive, working an average of thirty-five hours per week.

WORK EXPERIENCE

Sales Administrator

1998 – Present   Kent H. Landsberg Co.   San Marcos, CA

- Promoted from customer service representative responsible for providing exceptional customer service to build and maintain positive working relationships.
- Serve in a technical role helping to develop and support a new National Account Program that strategically supports our biggest customers producing over $12M in revenues annually.
- Assist Regional Vice President of Distribution effectively by handling a wide variety of situations and conflicts involving clerical and administrative tasks.
- Act as database administrator for IBM Leveraged Procurement, SalesLOGIX, and D&B Family Tree Finder.
- Manage multiple projects designed to improve customer satisfaction.

Summer Internship – Deputy Assistant Secretary of the Air Force for Science, Technology, and Engineering

2001   Department of Defense, Pentagon   Washington, DC

- Helped execute daily operations at Headquarters Directorate for sixty-two scientists, engineers, and administrative personnel.
- Assisted in ensuring policies and strategies of Deputy Assistant Secretary (DAS) were carried out effectively and in a timely manner.
- Reviewed correspondence and briefing materials for content and format to receive DAS approval.
- Interacted with staff of Assistant Secretary of the Air Force, Department of Defense, Congress, and White House.

KARA DUGGINS

Summer Internship – Manpower and Training Office
1998   *GTE Government Systems Corp.*   *Edwards AFB, CA*
- Interacted with both governmental and contractor personnel.
- Established and maintained personnel file system and database composed of mostly "Official Use Only" documents and handled accordingly.
- Conducted inventory on lab materials and compared against database; corrected discrepancies when applicable.
- Created and modified spreadsheets and office correspondence, entered a variety of forms in Jet Form Flow, and performed standard secretarial functions.

COMPUTER SKILLS

- Proficient using Windows XP/NT/2000/98/95
- Advanced proficiency with Microsoft Word, Excel, PowerPoint, Access, Publisher, and Outlook
- Trained Administrator for IBM Leveraged Procurement Services, SalesLogix, and Dunn & Bradstreet's Family Tree Finder
- Frequent user of JD Edwards AS/400 Sales Software

SAMPLE COVER LETTER

John Wiskosky

8738 Graceland Avenue Escondido, CA 92026	Home Phone: (760) 123-4567 Cell Phone: (760) 987-6543 Email: theking@hotmail.com

March 10, 2007

Mr. Tom Jones
Manager, Loan Department
San Diego Financial
444 E. Main Street
San Diego, CA 92123

Dear Mr. Jones,

While viewing the employment section of San Diego Financial's website, I noticed a need for a position as a Credit Manager. My experience with personal credit and loans, coupled with the near completion of a B.S. in Business Administration degree allows me to bring significant knowledge and experience to the job at hand. Please consider me for the Credit Manager position, as I would be an asset to San Diego Financial.

This position identified a number of requirements and my qualifications perfectly match the requirements listed.

YOUR REQUIREMENTS	MY QUALIFICATIONS
1. BA/BS Degree in Business or related field.	1. B.S in Business Administration with an emphasis in finance, May 2007.
2. Proven track record of goal achievement.	2. Continually depended on to deliver numerous sales at each job, in addition to obtaining financing for clients.
3. Leadership or sales experience preferred.	3. Five years of sales experience and four years of management experience.
4. Self-motivated	4. Highly motivated and looking to make a positive impact.

I am confident in my ability to make a positive contribution to San Diego Financial. I am enclosing my resume for further review. If you have any questions or would like additional information, please contact me at theking@hotmail.com or by phone at (760) 123-4567 (home) or (760) 987-6543 (cell). I will contact you next week to request an interview. Thank you for your time and consideration in reviewing my application.

Sincerely,

John Wiskosky

John Wiskosky

Who Is in Your Traveling Party?
Networking

DILBERT: © Scott Adams/Dist. by United Feature Syndicate, Inc.

Your success in attaining the summit of Mount Career hinges to a significant extent on *who* is in your traveling party. The common adage "It's not what you know but who you know that matters" is largely true when it comes to getting your foot in the door and generating solid job leads. So ask yourself a couple of difficult questions: Am I a networker extraordinaire (remember the New American Professional suggested by Tom Peters in Chapter 4)? How many people are spreading positive word-of-mouth advertising about my brand? With whom do I consult for professional advice and guidance? Members of your traveling party, or professional network, can come from any number of sources (e.g., immediate and extended family members, employers, professors, friends, religious affiliations, extracurricular organizations, etc.). This chapter describes the fundamental concept and power of networking, and then suggests several specific strategies to assist you in creating and expanding your network. It concludes with guidelines for obtaining professional references and letters of recommendation.

NETWORKING FUNDAMENTALS

Definition

Some career development experts take a more narrow view when defining networking, such as "networking refers to the process of developing and maintaining contacts."[1] While contacts are an important element in networking, I define *networking* as **the initiation and cultivation of mutually supportive, business-related relationships.** Dr. Moses elaborates on this view of networking and how it counteracts one of the frequently cited concerns about this process:

> Perhaps, like many people, you're uncomfortable about networking. Perhaps you think of it as being manipulative and exploitative—*using* other people to help you get ahead. Or perhaps you feel it is somehow unseemly for you as a professional to have to "schmooze" or "glad-hand." You think of networking as fundamentally insincere—feigning interest in someone when all you really want is to use them for your own ends.
>
> Networking is about more than glad-handing, "using people," or handing someone your business card as soon as you are introduced. Indeed many of the most effective networkers don't even bother with their business cards. Simply put, networking is about developing *mutually supportive relationships*. It is as much about being there for someone else as about "using" someone else to get ahead.[2]

Networking is *not* attending every social event. It is *not* contacting members in your network only when you need a job. It is *not* collecting business cards. Effective networkers are sincere in their interest of other people and what they do in their careers. They look for ways to help others professionally, or perhaps, how to achieve some mutually beneficial outcomes from a relationship.

The Power of Networking

How powerful is networking? The most common indicator applied to networking is finding new job leads. Studies typically report that 65 to 75% of all jobs found in the United States are obtained through networking.[3] Why is this process so effective in landing new jobs? Here are three main reasons:

1. Employers prefer hiring people they know personally or who are referred to them by someone they know and trust.

2. Networking expands your search party for that next job; you can naturally come to a knowledge of more opportunities as more people know what you are looking for.

3. Networking builds social capital, and like other forms of capital (such as financial and human), when managed effectively social capital brings a higher return on investment.

---

[1] Sukiennik, D., Bendat, W., & Raufman, L. (2007). *The career fitness program: Exercising your options* (8th ed.). Upper Saddle River, NJ: Pearson Prentice Hall, p. 248.

[2] Moses, B. (1998). *Career intelligence.* San Francisco: Berrett-Koehler Publishers, p. 174.

[3] See both Clark, T. (2000). *Career strategies.* Belmont, CA: South-Western College Publishing, Chapter 1; and Levitt, J. G. (2000). *Your career: How to make it happen.* Belmont, CA: South-Western College Publishing, Chapter 5.

However, you should not think of networking only in terms of "getting a job." It also has the potential to create new business opportunities, to provide new customers, to offer solutions to organizational problems, and to assist in your professional development. Don't view networking as something you just do when job hunting. Networking is an ongoing activity and it requires constant hard work to cultivate those relationships to the point where they are fruitful for both parties. In many ways, effective networking involves a mentality to continually learn, a sincere desire to help others, plus a healthy dose of communication skills (especially listening). Trust and confidence in your network members is essential. The following observation by Krakauer conveys similarities between climbing and networking (though the consequences are of different magnitude):

> In climbing, having confidence in your partners is no small concern. One climber's actions can affect the welfare of the entire team. The consequences of a poorly tied knot, a stumble, a dislodged rock, or some other careless deed are as likely to be felt by the perpetrator's colleagues as the perpetrator. Hence it's not surprising that climbers are typically wary of joining forces with those whose bona fides are unknown to them.[4]

You can do this. You *must* do this! I am not saying that you need to have a network of 200 people to achieve business success. But you will not climb your career mountain without critical assistance from others along the way.

NETWORKING STRATEGIES

When David Bennett and I created the "In the Executive's Chair" course, we purposefully included a question that was asked of each executive: "What role has networking and mentoring played in your career?" Out of 43 executives that visited in my tenure teaching the course, 42 stressed the vital importance of networking for career success. From their numerous comments and ideas, I have put together the following list of specific networking strategies. This should provide you with several options you can use depending on your preferences and the situation at hand.

- *List of 10.* Pepper de Callier, Chairman of Prague-based Bubenik Partners and former partner of Heidrick & Struggles, offered this unique approach that combines networking and the job search. He said to take a sheet of paper or index card and write down a list of 10 organizations in which you have an interest. Then as you interact with members of your network, you pull out the list and hand it to the person and ask, "Who do you know in any of these organizations?" Chances are the person will not know someone in all 10 organizations but will be able to identify at least a couple of contact points to refer you to within those potential employers. This approach has worked with executives in their search processes for different jobs. It works because it helps your network members focus their concentration on a narrow list of companies. If you just come up to a network member and ask, "Do you know of any job openings right now?" it will be

[4] Krakauer, J. (1997). *Into thin air.* New York: Doubleday, p. 47.

difficult for that person to help you because your question is so broad. One key to the effectiveness of this approach is the extent to which you have researched the 10 organizations to ensure a good fit.

- *Rounds at the table.* Ted Owen, former president and publisher of the *San Diego Business Journal* and current CEO of the Carlsbad Chamber of Commerce, explained his networking approach at social events. First, Ted doesn't hang around with the people he knows really well. If you are like me at all, that already makes you a little nervous, you really have to step beyond your comfort zone to emulate Ted. If the event is open seating, Ted will choose a table where he doesn't know anyone. He selects a chair and puts down his materials, then proceeds to take his business cards around the table to introduce himself to each person. As the meal proceeds he focuses on the two people sitting on either side of him. He listens to them and learns about their businesses and personal backgrounds. Keep in mind that essential to his professional roles is to know the pulse of the business community. He has to network profusely—and he does. The final icing on the cake from Ted is that he will send a follow-up e-mail (or handwritten note in some cases) the next morning to the two people he sat next to at the event the previous evening.

- *Internal and external networking.* Denise Fletcher, chief financial officer of MasterCard International, clarified the difference between internal and external networking. Denise indicated that she never was one to do a lot of external networking (supportive business-related relationships outside of your own work organization), or "schmoozing at professional functions" as she put it. What she did really well was networking within her own companies. This internal networking allowed her to gain consensus from across MasterCard when tough financial decisions needed to be resolved. She could talk the language of different functional areas and understand their unique problems. Her mantra was that you need to build bridges to others in your organization if you work with a larger company. I completely agree with her.

- *Surprise! Suppliers.* Did you ever think of your suppliers (or customers for that matter) as potential network members or mentors? Barbara Friedman, former president and cofounder of a technology publishing company and now an angel investor,[5] "supplied" this unique insight (pun intended—you laughed, right?). Good suppliers come to know your business almost as well as you do. Relationships between suppliers and customers can often generate new insights and occasionally, new employment opportunities.

- *Industry and professional associations.* Many executives expressed the importance of being well-connected in their respective industries and/or professions. Two of the most emphatic messages came from Bruce Nichols (former CEO of Formulabs, a company subsequently purchased in the late

---

[5] Wikipedia defines an *angel investor* as "an affluent individual who provides capital for a business start-up, usually in exchange for ownership equity. Unlike venture capitalists, angels typically do not manage the pooled money of others in a professionally managed fund. However, angel investors often organize themselves into angel networks or angel groups to share research and pool their own investment capital." The article can be accessed at http://en.wikipedia.org/wiki/Angel_investor.

1990s by Kimberly Clark), and Rich Sulpizio (former COO and president of Qualcomm). One of the reasons that this networking strategy is so helpful is that it conveys something easily defined about your brand. Rich is a telecommunications guru. Competitors in the telecommunications industry know him and his abilities. They know what he has helped Qualcomm accomplish, and he is well-respected. So if you are new to an industry or are considering changing industries or professions, find out what local, national, and international associations are relevant. If you are a student, check and see what local chapters of professional associations exist at your institution and get involved with one of them. The Internet can also help you find this information. Conducting informational interviews with seasoned members of specific industries or occupations will lead to an understanding of which associations are most valuable for your particular career aspirations.

- *Leave every job on good footing.* Former San Diego Entrepreneur of the Year Ken Olson reminded us to never burn past bridges. He said that an overlooked part of networking is former bosses and coworkers, and that you "should always leave every job on good footing with your employer." How do you follow this advice? It means that you never, *never* speak negatively about a previous or current employer or boss in an interview. It means that when you commit to a job offer with another company, you give your current employer sufficient notice (at least two weeks). It means that you follow the Boy Scout rule for campsite maintenance and leave your existing job in better shape than when you started.

- *Networking diversity.* Helen Adams, a partner at Deloitte & Touche, said part of her networking success has involved reaching out and cultivating relationships with individuals who are very different from herself. A scholar named Mark Granovetter published a landmark study in 1973 that showed the value of Helen's approach.[6] He conveyed the value of weak ties in personal networks. Strong ties are relationships with people who have high-frequency interaction and considerable social similarity. Weak ties are valuable because you learn of different opportunities and information. Think about it. If your network consists of six people who came from the same university, share the same fundamental beliefs in life, know the same people, attend the same social events, then the end result is that you all know roughly the same information. Look for people who bring a very different perspective or skill set to the table than you do. Broad networks are probably more important than deep networks.

- *Start networking with your classmates.* Bob Sporrer, former president of Rancho Santa Fe Bank, made a most impressive illustration when he visited our class. He told the students to start networking right now with the people in the class. To emphasize the point, he explained to the class that he knew of my alma mater and that the Cincinnati Reds were one of my favorite sports teams. He had taken the time to go out on the Internet and

---

[6] Granovetter, M. (1973). The strength of weak ties. *American Journal of Sociology, 78*(6), 1360–1380.

find my personal Web page. He is the only executive who ever did that. He knew the names of various students in the class without having ever met them. Do you understand the effect that preparation on his part had on the students and on David and me? Make the time to learn about other students in your courses and coworkers in your organizations. They may become future team members or business partners.

- *Networking? We don't know Jack!* Jack Hayes, founder of the Chairmen's RoundTable organization, claimed that he never bought into the idea of networking in his career. He stated that he never had really "done" networking. "I always believed that my hard work and performance would stand on its own merits," he said. Of course, the organization he founded has a strong networking feel to it and David still argues that Jack is one of the biggest networkers around. For Jack, it was never an intentional, or self-serving, process. He just likes to talk to people and learn about them.

- *Elevator pitch.* Regina Coffman, entrepreneur in the nutrition and fitness industry, emphasized the importance of having a concise and compelling elevator pitch to use while networking. The elevator pitch is your 1 to 2 minute explanation of what your company does, or what you do when applied to your career. Remember Brand You!

Most of these strategies concentrate on building your network. However, equally important is cultivating your network. David has done this incredibly well over the years. Think of what it takes to cultivate a first-rate garden. You need to plant some seeds. Those are the initial contacts you make. Then those seeds need some water. Water is the repeated interaction over the years, with you sometimes helping and other times being helped. Sunlight is essential. Warmth and true friendship should develop in these relationships. David does an excellent job of remembering key members of his network. He sends out birthday and anniversary cards, personal notes, and other items to commemorate important events. He will call a member of his network just to ask how the person is doing. There are no strings attached in these relationships. And yes, you have to remove some weeds from time to time. There may be some relationships that grow distant or turn sour for whatever reason. It is also possible, however remote, that you may need to apply just a little fertilizer to prepare the ground for networking seeds that will grow.

 **TREK TASK 14**
BUILDING YOUR NETWORK

Start with 10 contacts. They can be family members, friends, classmates, work associates, and professional contacts. Starting now (if you haven't prior to this class), build a database or spreadsheet that contains the key information (contact info, organization, title, type of assistance they can provide) about your network members. Start today!

PROFESSIONAL REFERENCES AND RECOMMENDATION LETTERS

You will likely need to provide two documents at some point during your career that provide written evidence of what members of your traveling party think of you. The first document is a one-page sheet with names and contact information of three to five professional references. The second document consists of recommendation letters from the professional references who know you best. Remember one of the résumé guidelines discussed in Chapter 5: Avoid putting a note about references on your résumé because it is unnecessary. However, you do need to have a one-page sheet of professional references prepared to give to prospective employers, either during an initial interview or when completing a job application. Here are some guidelines to help you obtain these two documents professionally and effectively.

Choosing Professional References

Beyond being drawn from your larger pool of network contacts, the three to five individuals you select as your professional references should meet the following criteria:

- They should think highly of your capabilities (i.e., be willing to give you a strong recommendation).
- They should have knowledge of your performance track record and best qualities.
- They should be credible (this is usually based on their titles and organizational affiliations).
- They should *not* be relatives.

It is better if you have more than three individuals who meet these criteria. There are some additional considerations to think about when choosing which individuals you will put on your references list. If you are applying to graduate school programs, you will usually be requested to provide references and/or letters of recommendations from three persons. Typically, one or two of those persons should be in academic positions, so you will need to think about your professors and which of them could provide a positive recommendation on your behalf. It is always a good idea to have a professional in the industry or occupational field for which you are applying. This reference will usually have added credibility to a prospective employer. It is acceptable to use a former boss as a reference as long as you left that previous employment on positive footing. You have to be careful about using former employers as references though, as the following comments by Anne Fisher illustrate:

> "[T]he problem here stems from a recent rash of big nasty lawsuits against ex-employers who allegedly gave out false or otherwise flawed data about employees who had left. Many companies are now so leery of being sued (again) that they hesitate to reveal anything at all about anybody. So prospective employers are extremely limited in what they can find out about you from your old boss. Just about the only two questions that

won't get anyone in legal hot water are 'Was this person in your employ?' along with a few factual details like the dates you worked there and what your title was, and 'Would you rehire this person if you had the chance?' "[7]

The second question is the litmus test question. If you believe your former boss would say "no" or even "maybe" to that rehire question, then you should absolutely *not* consider that person as a professional reference. Given these caveats, carefully choose the three to five individuals who can give you the most positive, specific, and credible recommendations. The information about these individuals should be placed on your References page in this format (or something close to it):

Troy Nielson, Ph.D.
Associate Professor of Management
Utah Valley State College
800 W. University Parkway
Orem, UT 84058-5999
(801) 863-8235
nielsotr@uvsc.edu

This format provides all necessary information for a prospective employer to contact your reference via e-mail, snail mail, or telephone. It also gives your reference's title and organizational affiliation, which can enhance the reference's credibility.

Interacting with Your References

Rule number one is to always ask permission of those individuals you would like to have serve as professional references—always! Make sure that they know what your job and career aspirations are and that they have the time to respond to inquiries by your prospective employers. On a couple of occasions in the past three years I have received a phone call or e-mail from an organization about a former student who has listed me (without my knowledge) as a reference. I will still try to answer those inquiries, but I am neither as well-prepared to talk about the student's qualifications nor think as highly of those students because of their lack of professional courtesy. Even if your reference tells you that you can use his or her name anytime, it is still a good policy to alert your references when you are interviewing for positions.

It is also important for you to maintain contact periodically with those professional references, even if you are not actively seeking new employment. Keep them posted on your current position, career ambitions, and major accomplishments. These individuals may even be considered as your board of directors—keep them informed and help them as you have the capacity to do so.

---

[7] Fisher, A. (2001). *If my career's on the fast track, where do I get a road map?* New York: William Morrow, p. 182.

Obtaining Letters of Recommendation

In some situations you will be asked to provide letters of recommendation as part of your application process. This is especially true for applications to graduate programs. Your references are good candidates for these letters but keep in mind the following guidelines:

- If the letter is for a specific application process that has a deadline, inform your references a sufficient time (ideally, at least two weeks) before the deadline.

- When you ask someone to provide a recommendation letter on your behalf, give them all the needed information—purpose (specific position or program for which you are applying), program or position description, current version of your resume, time frame for completion (when do you need the letter?), and any other specific instructions from the organization that has requested the recommendation letters.

- Make sure you understand whether the letter should be returned to you or sent directly to the requesting organization; communicate that information to those providing the recommendation letters.

- If you gave your references substantial lead time before the application deadline, send them a gentle follow-up reminder (3–5 days before the deadline) just to ensure that they have completed and sent your letter.

Under some circumstances, you may request a more generic letter of recommendation from a professor or a soon-to-be former employer just to have in your files, and to use in the near future should the need arise. You should still follow the guidelines above, with the understanding that the deadline is more flexible.

 TREK TASK 15

PROFESSIONAL REFERENCES PAGE

Complete your references page. Use the format suggested in this chapter and create a one-page sheet with the names of three to five professional references. Make sure that before actually using these references in job searches that you have obtained permission from these individuals and that they are willing to serve you in this capacity.

Now that you have your passport (résumé and cover letter) in better shape and have identified some key members of your traveling party, we are ready to explore possible routes up the mountain. Prepare yourself to start researching different career paths and to map key steps for your ascent along those paths.

▲🚶🚶 TREK LIST

- ☐ **NETWORKING**   The initiation and cultivation of mutually supportive, business-related relationships.

- ☐ **NETWORKING STRATEGIES**   I have identified one of the provided networking strategies that I can apply to enhance my professional network right now.

- ☐ **BASE 10**   I have created a database or spreadsheet with names and contact information of at least 10 persons who are supportive of my career aspirations. They will form the base, or foundation, of my network.

- ☐ **REFERENCES**   I have identified three to five professional references, obtained their permission to serve as references, and documented their contact information on a one-page References document.

Researching the Corporate Terrain

On May 22, 1963, Tom Hornbein, a thirty-two-year-old doctor from Missouri, and Willi Unsoeld, thirty-six, a professor of theology from Oregon, reached the summit of Everest via the peak's daunting West Ridge, previously unclimbed. By then the summit had already been achieved on four occasions, by eleven men, but the West Ridge was considerably more difficult than either of the two previously established routes: the South Col and Southeast Ridge or the North Col and Northeast Ridge. Hornbein's and Unsoeld's ascent was—and continues to be—deservedly hailed as one of the great feats in the annals of mountaineering.

—*Jon Krakauer (Into Thin Air, pp. 21–22)*

Unlike Everest, reaching the career summit is a dynamic process that consists of myriad potential career routes. Although there are many routes, you should commit yourself to the same rigor in researching those routes as the mountaineers who seek the top of Everest. While specific career paths are unique to each individual, there are three general categories of career paths that deserve our immediate attention. The first major category is the corporate path. This chapter explains the why, what, where, when, and how of researching corporate destinations. Chapter 8 will discuss two other broad career routes—the entrepreneurial path and the graduate school path.

WHY RESEARCH YOUR ROUTES?

How would you like to give yourself a big competitive advantage over other applicants for a given position? Pay close attention to the following statistic: "Employers nationwide say applicants who research employers well *increase their employability as much as 25 percent.*"[1]

---

[1] Levitt, J. G. (2000). *Your career: How to make it happen,* Belmont, CA: South-Western Educational Publishing, p. 108.

But isn't the purpose of the hiring process for the employer to research your qualifications to see if you are the right person for the job? Yes! So how does diligent research of a company give you a 25% edge? There are six important reasons you should carefully research each new step on your route up Mount Career:

1. To answer the interview question, Why do you want to work here?
2. To shine throughout the hiring process
3. To make career decisions resulting in a better fit
4. To improve your marketing capacity
5. To compensate for less industry or work experience
6. To increase self-confidence

Why Do You Want to Work Here?

This is a common question asked of applicants in an initial job interview. Interviewers usually ask this question for two reasons—to uncover some of your motives and to see if you did your homework about the company. Employers want to know early in the hiring process if there is a good fit between what an applicant seeks and what the employer can provide. Employers also want to know how much research you have done on their companies so they can assess your level of genuine interest.

Let me give you a concrete example. When we conducted a hiring process for new faculty members at Cal State San Marcos, this question (or a similar variation) almost always occurred in the initial interview. Suppose the faculty candidate responded by stressing his research activities and the desire to conduct large research studies with the assistance of doctoral students. I know two things very quickly. First, this person's motives did *not* fit very well with what we could offer. The CSU system gives first priority to teaching and second priority to research (well, it can feel like a third priority sometimes, but that is for another book), unlike at major research institutions. Second, the candidate's response reflects minimal understanding of our institution, basic knowledge that could have been captured to some degree by spending even a few minutes on the College of Business Web site. No doctoral program existed then, and none exists now. This question quickly separated those applicants who were not serious about taking a position at our institution. It is not surprising that many people just want a paid trip to San Diego in November or February (our heaviest recruiting months). You must give thought to this question before your interview, perhaps even before you submit a resume to the company. *I suggest you commit to memory at least three specific reasons for your interest in each prospective employer.*

Shining in the Hiring Process

Conducting thorough company research starts to pay off in the cover letter at the beginning of the hiring process. Then it will help you in several aspects of the job interview. First, you will be able to respond intelligently to questions about the company. For example, let's suppose you were applying for a marketing position and the interviewer asked you the following: "What changes would you make to improve our marketing strategies?" Only solid research efforts will help you pass that test! Second, if you were able to discover in advance the identity of your interviewers, you might be able to learn more about their backgrounds, areas of expertise, and so forth. Establishing some rapport and common ground with the interviewers is an effective strategy. Finally, research assists you in forming thought-provoking, specific questions about the company. Furthermore, research on salaries will help you through the final step of negotiating an offer successfully.

Making High-Fit Career Decisions

Researching companies in advance may save time and money for both you and those companies by avoiding poor-fit situations. Remember the Person–Job Fit model? (I told you it would be wise to commit this model to memory.) You cannot make well-informed career decisions without knowing what the position demands and what incentives the company provides to employees upon meeting those demands. Make sure that you know what you want—at least the essential criteria. Then it is your responsibility to examine the company thoroughly to assess the fit.

Improving Your Marketing Capacity

Understanding a company's biggest challenges, its needs, and its competitive industry position enables you to present a more compelling case for the value you would add to that organization. What do we learn from Marketing 101? Understand your customer's needs! Think of prospective employers as potential customers, and you are trying to sell them something unique—*yourself*. Make the time to learn their strengths, weaknesses, key competitors, and so forth.

 TREK TASK 16

CONDUCT SWOT ANALYSIS ON PROSPECTIVE EMPLOYERS

Want to blow your interviewer away with your research? When you identify an organization you really want to work for, conduct your own SWOT (Strengths, Weaknesses, Opportunities, Threats) analysis on that organization. Send your completed analysis to an appropriate organizational member and/or bring it with you to the job interview.

Compensating for Inexperience

Knowing more about an industry or a company can help you make inroads when you are changing careers to areas in which you have minimal experience. You need to at least be able to "talk the talk" by having a solid knowledge of industry trends, challenges, and terminology. In some occupations, having done ample research will not overcome lack of experience or formal credentials (e.g., physician, pilot), but you give yourself a better shot by showing how serious you are about the company and demonstrating your capacity to grasp new concepts.

Increasing Self-Confidence

There is an old adage that says, "Preparation precedes power." The more you know your subject matter the higher your confidence in the ability to articulate your ideas and show the company how you can contribute to reaching its objectives. If possible, do your research over time rather than trying to cram it in the hour before your scheduled interview. Employers are looking for confident, assertive employees. Doing exceptional research on the company will give you that edge.

WHAT INFORMATION NEEDS TO BE RESEARCHED?

The following six information categories need to be researched. I have suggested specific data that you should obtain for each of the categories. It is important to note that you don't need to research all six categories for every job search. For example, if you love your occupation but were just the victim of a company layoff, you will not need to research occupations. These six categories represent the broad spectrum of information needed for those who don't know what path they want to take.

- *Occupations.* Occupational families (major occupational clusters); future growth trends; necessary credentials (degrees and/or certifications); professional associations and key networking groups; any structured career paths; and general salary ranges.
- *Industries.* Current issues and future trends (including growth outlook); major products and services; industry leaders and competitive positions; professional associations and/or publications; general salary ranges; and geographical hotbeds, if any.
- *Companies.* Key products and services; geographical locations; number of employees; projected growth; leaders; culture (core values); major competitors; financial stability; organizational structure; available positions; and employee benefits.
- *Terminology.* Common jargon; buzzwords or initiatives (e.g., Six Sigma); important acronyms; and business vocabulary.
- *Specific positions.* Actual job descriptions; required and preferred qualifications; reporting relationships; prioritized objectives; salary and benefits information.
- *Hiring process/interviewers.* Key steps in the hiring process; estimated time frame for making a hiring decision; important decision makers involved in the process; type of interview (e.g., telephone, one-on-one, panel).

WHERE CAN THE INFORMATION BE FOUND?

Overall, *your two best sources for information related to your career-related research are the Internet and members of your professional network.* You should tap those two sources constantly during any job transition period. The following table provides other sources you should use to obtain data for the six categories identified in the previous section.

SOURCE	SUGGESTIONS OR COMMENTS
Current or former employees	Outstanding source for several data items, including: necessary credentials; professional associations, networking groups, and publications; possible career paths; most aspects of company information (especially culture); terminology and buzzwords; and steps in the hiring process.
Occupational Outlook Handbook (OOH)	This information is annually compiled and produced by the U.S. Department of Labor, Bureau of Labor Statistics. It is usually available in hard copy at university career centers and always accessible online (www.bls.gov); the premier nonpeople source for occupational data. (See Exhibits 7.1 and 7.2 on pages 80–82 for examples of the detailed information that the Bureau of Labor Statistics provides about occupations and industries in the United States.)
Company Web sites	These provide you with most of the company information. However, you should remember that the company controls the information that appears on the Web site. Much of the information will be factual in nature and accurate, but you should verify cultural values, projected growth, and financial stability through other sources.
Business publications	Key information on industry and overall business trends; terminology and buzzwords; companies (best to work for, most admired, fastest growing, etc.); and professional associations. Commonly used business publications include *BusinessWeek, Fast Company, Forbes, Fortune, Inc.,* and the *Wall Street Journal.*
Internet	So much information, so little time! Search engines and various online resources can be used to provide a considerable amount of the data for each of the categories except the hiring process. A listing of helpful Web sites can be found at the end of this chapter in Exhibit 7.3.

Network members   While the Internet gives you fast, surface-level data about your career choices, your networking contacts can supplement that data with personal insights and depth. Make your aspirations known to key members of your professional network. Identify members who have experience in the occupations, industries, or companies that are of interest to you. If no such network members exist, ask them who they know that works in your desired occupation or at your preferred company. If you still are not coming into contact with the right sources to become well-informed, you may need to purposefully expand your network to include someone with the necessary information.

EXHIBIT 7.1
TWENTY-THREE STANDARD OCCUPATIONAL CLASSIFICATION MAJOR GROUPS

Occupational Group	2005 Mean Annual Wage
Management	$88,450
Business and financial operations	57,930
Computer and mathematical	67,100
Architecture and engineering	63,910
Life, physical, and social science	58,030
Community and social services	37,530
Legal	81,070
Education, training, and library	43,450
Arts, design, entertainment, sports, and media	44,310
Health care practitioners and technical	59,170
Health care support	23,850
Protective service	35,750
Food preparation and serving related	17,840
Building and grounds cleaning and maintenance	21,930
Personal care and service	22,180
Sales and related	32,800
Office and administrative support	29,710

Continued

Occupational Group	2005 Mean Annual Wage
Farming, fishing, and forestry	21,010
Construction and extraction	38,260
Installation, maintenance, and repair	38,050
Production	29,890
Transportation and material moving	28,820
Military specific	27,220

Source: From *Occupational Employment Statistics,* U.S. Department of Labor, Bureau of Labor Statistics Web site (www.bls.gov/oes/).

EXHIBIT 7.2
CAREER GUIDE TO INDUSTRIES

Professional and business services

Advertising and public relations services

Computer systems design and related services

Employment, scientific, and technical consulting services

Management, scientific, and technical consulting services

Scientific research and development services

Education and health services

Child-care services

Educational services

Health care

Social assistance

Leisure and hospitality

Arts, entertainment, and recreation

Food services and drinking places

Hotels and other accommodations

Trade

Automobile dealers

Clothing, accessory, and general merchandise stores

Grocery stores

Wholesale trade

Finance activities

Banking

Insurance

Securities, commodities, and investments

Continued

Manufacturing	Information
Aerospace manufacturing	Broadcasting
Chemicals manufacturing	Internet service providers, Web search portals, and data processing services
Computer and electronic product manufacturing	Motion picture and video
Food manufacturing	Publishing (nonsoftware)
Machinery manufacturing	Software publishers
Motor vehicle and parts manufacturing	Telecommunications
Pharmaceutical and medicine manufacturing	**Government**
Printing	Advocacy, grantmaking, and civic organizations
Steel manufacturing	Federal government, excluding the Postal Service
Textile and apparel manufacturing	State and local government, except education and health
Transportation and utilities	**Agriculture, mining, and construction**
Air transportation	Agriculture, forestry, and fishing
Utilities	Construction
Truck transportation and warehousing	Mining
	Oil and gas extraction

Source: Based on *2006–2007 Career Guide to Industries,* U.S. Department of Labor, Bureau of Labor Statistics (www.bls.gov/oco/cg).

WHEN SHOULD YOU CONDUCT THE RESEARCH?

The quick answer to this question is that you should continuously hone your knowledge of your current occupation, industry, and company as well as its key competitors. When considering job or career changes, the first four categories should be researched as much as possible before applying for specific jobs, while the fifth category should be explored as you are applying for those jobs. The final category is only relevant as you obtain actual interviews.

How Should You Conduct the Research?

Suffering from information overload? Too many routes that sound interesting? Here are a few tips that will help you maximize your research effectiveness:

- Conduct informational interviews
- Obtain referrals
- Develop a research tracking system
- Spend focused time on the Internet
- Practice the art of following up

Conduct Informational Interviews

One of the best methods to gather current information about potential career paths is to conduct an informational interview with someone having expertise in the career path you're investigating. In some of my classes I require that students conduct such an interview. In my own professional development I continue to conduct informational interviews. I almost always learn something new and significant. A positive thing about informational interviews is that the interviewee feels minimal pressure and therefore will usually speak candidly and openly in response to the interviewer's questions. Most professionals are willing to talk about their experiences and work activities for 30 minutes if given enough notice. Some quick tips are (a) identify two or three individuals who can provide the information you seek (in case one of them is unavailable); (b) extend professional courtesy to the interviewee (remember you want something from him or her); (c) prepare a set of questions beforehand and take them with you to the interview; and (d) obtain any referrals from the interviewee before leaving.

Obtain Referrals

Before you conclude any informational interview or, for that matter, any conversation with one of your network members, you should ask the referral question: "Do you know someone else I should talk with about this occupation?" (or this industry, this company, etc.). Remember that informational interviews are valuable not only for the content knowledge they provide but for the social connections they provide. We lose a major opportunity to expand our knowledge base and our network when we neglect to ask for a referral.

Develop a Research Tracking System

If you are a "fly by the seat of your pants" type of decision maker this suggestion will probably annoy you. And if your job search is very targeted (meaning that only one or two organizations are on your radar), then this step is not necessary.

But if you are casting a wider net you will want to use some of our omnipresent technology to track your research and eventually your job search process. I prefer an Excel spreadsheet to track what I have done. My approach is to list the potential organizations, industries, and occupations down the left-hand side as rows of the spreadsheets. My columns then become key research steps I want to track, such as relevant Web sites, checking with my network members, talking with organizational members, and using any other method that helps you learn more. Research is hard work, but it leads to better interviews, more informed career decisions, and increased peace of mind.

Spend Focused Time on the Internet

The Internet provides us with much information that can help us in our research of prospective employers. Remember, though, that it is called the Web for several reasons. One reason is that we can easily become distracted and ensnared in the mass of information at our disposal. Make sure you use your time wisely. In fact, I recommend that you have two or three specific research objectives in mind before you start surfing the Internet. When you do find Web pages that provide helpful information, be sure to either print the page or at least save the Web page in your Favorites list on your browser. I can tell you that I have neglected to do this several times, and it can be a big time waster and a source of frustration when you cannot find the Web site again.

Practice the Art of Following Up

Sometimes your research will lead you to an action that cannot be completed at that time. For example, you may be invited to join professional association, read a recent article in a trade publication, or contact someone else. When someone offers these opportunities to become more informed about your potential career path, you don't want this person to fall through the cracks of your busy life. Therefore, I suggest that you have a column in your research tracking system for "Next Steps." Put unresolved action items in that column and then review your tracking system regularly.

This chapter has offered you several practical strategies for researching career paths with existing organizations, also called the corporate path. These same steps will work with for-profit and not-for-profit organizations. I hope you are not feeling overwhelmed with the information because we have two more paths to consider in the next chapter—starting your own organization (entrepreneurial path) and furthering your education (graduate program path).

 **TREK TASK 17**

CAREER PATH CLARIFICATION

Based on your own preferences, some initial research, and Exhibits 7.1, 7.2, and 7.3, use the following chart page to list your preferences related to occupations, industries, and companies. What else do you still need to learn about these routes to make well-informed decisions? Where can you obtain this missing knowledge? Try to narrow your focus to no more than three potential career routes.

OCCUPATIONS   **INDUSTRIES**   **COMPANIES**

_____   _____   _____

_____   _____   _____

_____   _____   _____

TREK LIST

☐ **RESEARCH RULES**   Outshine other applicants by doing more thorough research of the organizations with which you desire to work. I know *six* reasons why research pays off.

☐ **WHAT, WHERE, WHEN, AND HOW**   For my three most appealing corporate paths, I have identified what information I need to obtain, where my best sources are for obtaining it, and how I can get it.

☐ **INFORMATIONAL INTERVIEW**   I have completed (or am scheduled to complete) an informational interview about one of my three potential paths.

EXHIBIT 7.3
KEY INTERNET RESEARCH SOURCES

Research Source	Internet Address
Career-related Web sites	
Monster	www.monster.com
CareerBuilder	www.careerbuilder.com
What Color Is Your Parachute?	www.jobhuntersbible.com
HotJobs	hotjobs.yahoo.com
Leading business periodicals	
Fast Company	www.fastcompany.com
Fortune	www.fortune.com
BusinessWeek	www.businessweek.com
Wall Street Journal	www.wsj.com
Forbes	www.forbes.com
Barron's	www.barrons.com
Business 2.0	www.business20.com
Inc.	www.inc.com
Business research/search engines	
Hoover's Online	www.hoovers.com
Google	www.google.com
Ask Jeeves	www.ask.com
Yahoo	www.yahoo.com
AltaVista	www.altavista.com
Metacrawler	www.metacrawler.com

Custom Routes
Entrepreneurial Endeavors and Graduate Glory

> Your time is limited, so don't waste it living someone else's life. Don't be trapped by dogma, which is living with the results of other people's thinking. Don't let the noise of others' opinions drown out your own inner voice. And most important, have the courage to follow your heart and intuition. They somehow already know what you truly want to become. Everything else is secondary.
>
> —*Steve Jobs*

So what if the corporate path doesn't appeal to you? There are two other fairly well-traveled routes up Mount Career: (a) going into business for yourself—being an entrepreneur; and (b) pursuing advanced degrees—being a graduate student. When considered along with the corporate path, these three paths are not mutually exclusive. For example, you might start your career with a Fortune 500 company and then start your own business. While you are running your own business you may decide that a graduate degree would facilitate your achievement of career goals. You can certainly follow two of these three paths simultaneously at least for a determined length of time. I haven't met too many individuals who have tried all three paths at once. Theoretically, it is possible, but each of the three paths is sufficiently time-consuming when considered alone.

Before I suggest some tips for success in each of these routes, it's time for some personal disclosure. I can speak from experience about graduate programs, especially graduate business programs. Surviving a doctoral program, teaching graduate students, serving on a graduate program committee, and benchmarking graduate programs allow me to share with you from personal experience the factors to consider when researching possible graduate programs. However, while I consider myself an avid "intrapreneur," I have never run my own business. My admiration for those who have made the risks and found success as entrepreneurs is very high. Whether that business is cleaning pools or starting your own computer company (à la Michael Dell), it doesn't matter. So what I share with you about the entrepreneurial path is based on insights from experts and from numerous discussions I have had with successful entrepreneurs.

So You Want to Be an Entrepreneur?

Remember your results from the CSMQ (Career Success Map Questionnaire) back in Chapter 3? Look at them again. How highly did you score on the Getting Free and Getting High dimensions? If you scored 8 or above on either orientation, you should consider an entrepreneurial path. If you scored 10 or higher on either one, you should definitely focus on starting your own organization in the near future. The purpose of this chapter is not to provide you with tips on how to be a successful entrepreneur. Instead, I want to share with you four strategies for deciding if this path is right for you.

1. Learn about successful entrepreneurs (through study and personal conversation).
2. Discuss the implications with those closest to you.
3. Test for fit with Brand You.
4. Create a skeleton business plan.

Learn about Successful Entrepreneurs

The same strategy of informational interviewing that I recommended for researching corporate paths applies to exploring entrepreneurial paths. You may want to start by talking with successful entrepreneurs in any type of business. Eventually you should home in on those who have been successful with a business similar to the one you are considering.

The following example given by Richard Bolles emphasizes this point:

> It is *mindboggling* how many people start a new business, at home or elsewhere, without ever talking to anybody else in the same kind of business. One job-hunter told me she started a homemade candle business, without ever talking to anyone else who had tried a similar endeavor. Her business went belly-up within a year and a half. She concluded: no one should go into such a business. I concluded: she hadn't done her homework, before she started.[1]

Not only will these individuals give you valuable information about their successes and failures, they may also become important members of your network. Beyond talking with entrepreneurs, read their stories. Study the approaches of great entrepreneurs. While no start-up experience is exactly the same, there are common stages and elements for which you can be better prepared by learning how others have succeeded and failed.

Discuss the Implications

The most positive estimates of new business-venture success rates are about 50% (the more typical figure is only 10 to 30%). Because of the potential for failure, it

---

[1] Bolles, R. N. (2002). *What color is your parachute?* Berkeley, CA: Ten Speed Press, p. 154.

is vital that you discuss what this path means to you and those closest to you. What will this path do to your level of stress? To your expected happiness? To your savings account? What will you do if the business doesn't succeed? What will happen if it does succeed? How will it affect your family or other nonwork activities? What is your best-case scenario? What is your worst-case scenario? What potential risks will you have to manage? Make sure that you are committed to the path and have the support of your family and closest friends. The path will be demanding and turbulent, but it can also be extremely rewarding.

Test with Brand You

Think about the brand message that you developed in Chapter 2. How does your new business idea fit with your current "brand"? Would going into business for yourself allow you to more fully leverage your unique talents and traits? Would your best skills be used more frequently? How passionate are you about the new business idea? Regardless of whether you are working in a corporation or for yourself, you want to stay true to your passions and best skills.

Create a Skeleton Business Plan

This is a time-consuming but essential preparatory activity for launching your own business. In the late 1990s, entrepreneurs could arrange a meeting with venture capitalists, show up, cough, and walk away with millions of dollars in financial backing. The dot-com crash has ended all of that. Most entrepreneurs who I have talked with in recent years agree that the biggest challenge for small start-up companies right now is to obtain the necessary financing to stay in business until they reach profitability. They have also cited that to receive any funding you absolutely must have a solid, thorough business plan. I suggest that even before you commit yourself to the path of starting your own organization, you should at least complete a basic business plan. Business Plan Pro or other software templates are available for relatively low costs to assist you in developing a business plan. Ask members of your network to review an executive summary of your business plan. Ask two or three of your closest professional friends to read the entire business plan and give you their honest assessments. The following lists several benefits for doing this early in your entrepreneurial path.

- The research will help you determine if this is a viable business or not.
- You learn the industry, key competitors, and customer markets, and identify potential marketing strategies.
- It will help you start to bridge the gulf from "idea" to "execution."
- It forces you to examine the financial implications and potential obstacles.
- You will have to do it sooner or later—so it might as well be sooner.

One more thing about traveling the entrepreneurial path that I need to share with you. I get the feeling too often from my students that they expect self-employment to be an easier path than working for someone else. According to the overwhelming majority of entrepreneurs with whom I have conversed about this subject, starting a successful new business is an enormous undertaking, more time-consuming, and often more stressful than a regular full-time position at an established company. While the sense of accomplishment and monetary rewards are potentially very high with the entrepreneurial path, don't think that it will free up more time in your day to enjoy leisure activities or to lounge around at home while your employees do the work.

TREK TASK 18
ENTREPRENEURIAL PROFILE

Do you have qualities that are consistent with those of successful entrepreneurs? Take one of the following online quizzes to see how you measure up.

www.e-magnify.com/envision/quiz.asp
www.venturecentre.on.ca/english/myventure/quiz.htm

SO YOU WANT ANOTHER DEGREE?

The first blunt question I need to ask you is *Why*? No, I am not trying to be sarcastic. I do believe that on average the more education a person obtains the better that person's opportunities. However, earning an advanced degree (meaning a masters or doctoral degree) should rarely be an end in and of itself. What is your objective? Will the degree improve your upward mobility within your current company? Is it a required credential for entry into a specific type of occupation or organization? Will the degree enhance your marketability? How important is the institution from which you earn the degree? Some employers care only that you have a masters degree. Others hire only graduates from specific programs. The graduate program path is, by nature, a temporary path. You cannot stay on this path for your entire working life, although I knew a couple of doctoral students who seemed to test that philosophy. Therefore, this path must be framed in the broader context of your overall career and your personal circumstances.

Several factors that you need to consider related to the graduate program path are

- *Timing.* How do you know when it's the right time to pursue an advanced degree?
- *Degree type.* Masters or doctorate, and content area.
- *Degree institution.* Choice of universities, including online providers.
- *Program type.* Traditional, part-time, professional, executive, distance learning.

- *Admission requirements.* Application deadlines, qualifying exams, recommendation letters, program requirements, and major steps in the application process.

Let's take each of these factors in greater depth and address some of the common decisions related to graduate programs.

Timing

There is no set answer to the issue of timing, but one thing is certain: enrollments in graduate programs increase during times of economic recession. Why? Lower opportunity costs. In many cases the pursuit of a graduate degree demands either reducing or completely eliminating one's full-time employment. Therefore, when the economy is poor, the opportunity cost of going back to school is lower.

Another issue related to timing is that certain programs may require specific timing relative to your graduation from your undergraduate program. For example, a masters degree program in biotechnology may require that students start in their undergraduate program, receiving a bachelor's degree in biology and then a masters degree one year later (a typical 5-year program). On the other hand, many MBA programs require that students have 3 or more years of professional work experience before they can be admitted into those programs. The purpose for this requirement is to allow individuals the opportunity to live in the business world for a few years. The concepts taught in an MBA program can then be analyzed and learned relative to actual professional experiences.

Even if the program you desire does not promote a specific entry time following your undergraduate program, you must weigh the pros and cons of entering a graduate program soon after you complete your undergraduate program. For example, among the pros are that you still have an academic mindset and taking the appropriate qualifying exam (GMAT, MCAT, LSAT, etc.) tends to be easier when formal education is fresh in your mind. Among the cons, burnout is the biggest problem; if you are tired of the relentless grind of formal education you may want to give yourself a mental refresher period. Lack of "real-world" experience may also hurt you when you are compared to your graduate program peers.

Finally, if you have a significant other and/or dependents, they must be included in the decision process. Graduate programs are typically very demanding, and spouse or family support is important for program success. When I was considering a Ph.D. in 1993, my wife and I had one child. Given our desire to have at least a couple more children, we decided it was best to start the doctoral program sooner rather than later when my job would need to provide for more dependents. Make sure that you weigh the trade-offs and sacrifices carefully. Also, don't forget to check with your employer to learn the company policy on tuition reimbursement. It may be worth earning that degree now when it will be paid for completely or partially by your employer.

Degree Type

Much of the decision about what degree program to pursue is based on your career objectives for earning an advanced degree in the first place. For most people who earn graduate degrees, they stop at the masters level (MS, MA, MBA). However, certain professions require a doctoral degree, such as university professors (Ph.D.), lawyers (J.D.), and physicians (M.D.).

The content area of the degree (business administration, physics, humanities, sociology, etc.) is completely up to you and your career aspirations. Just remember, though, that an advanced degree sends even stronger signals to prospective employers about positions for which you are qualified. You can become pigeonholed into certain types of positions, so choose wisely!

Degree Institution

Does the university that grants your degree really matter? Maybe. Probably. At least immediately after you earn the degree. It depends on whom you ask. In one of our Executive's Chair sessions, the president of an influential regional business publication asserted that the institution doesn't matter. Of course, he earned his degree from National University, which is considered by some employers and some academics as an inferior degree and institution. Later that semester, a partner in a local law firm was our guest executive. He had earned his law degree from Harvard. What do you think his perspective was on this issue? That's right! The institution makes a huge difference, he claimed, at least in the legal profession. My personal view is that degrees from the elite, most reputable schools in a particular discipline will generally lead to more open doors upon graduation than degrees from less prestigious institutions. Having said that, I should note three caveats: (a) those additional open doors may not be doors that you care about; (b) like the degree itself, the institution granting you the degree guarantees you nothing if you don't perform and manage your career effectively; and (c) stronger name recognition of a university does not necessarily mean a higher-quality learning experience.

In some cases, your degree type will narrow the field of potential institutions to consider. Try to identify the best institutions in your particular content area. For example, if you wanted to specialize in international business, the two most highly regarded programs are Thunderbird (the American Graduate School of International Management) and the University of South Carolina. Some specialized graduate programs may only exist at a small number of institutions.

Personal circumstances may point to an institution that may not necessarily be the highest in reputation. Let me illustrate with my choice of doctoral programs. When I applied for doctoral programs early in 1994, I applied to five programs. Within two months I was notified that I had been accepted for two of the programs: the University of Utah and the University of Washington. Both had reputable, internationally accredited business schools. Neither were in the top 20 business schools at the time, but both were in the top 75. The University of Washington probably had a slightly stronger reputation in academic circles in my discipline area of organizational behavior and human resources. However, my wife and

I mutually agreed that Utah's offer was the right one for us to accept. Proximity to family and cost of living were the two major factors in this decision. Neither of us regrets the decision. We would make the same decision again if we went back in time.

One more issue related to your choice of institution. Some employers will look at a graduate degree even more favorably if it was *not* earned at the same institution as the person's undergraduate degree. Again, some programs are set up as combined undergraduate–graduate programs and so that isn't really an option in those programs. When you pursue a graduate degree from the same university from which you earned your bachelor's degree, the advantage is familiarity—you know at least some of the professors, the campus layout, and how to get things done at that campus (a faster learning curve). The disadvantage is also familiarity—you miss out on the diversity of perspectives that a new group of faculty would provide; plus familiarity sometimes breeds complacency.

Program Type

Based on your professional and personal circumstances, you may opt for one of several types of programs. In the table that follows I briefly describe five common program types. Your choice of graduate programs may be strongly influenced by the type of program that you deem most feasible.

PROGRAM TYPE	DESCRIPTION OR COMMENTS
Traditional	These programs for full-time students take place during the daytime. Students typically give up their full-time employment to fulfill the program demands. Students are usually admitted in cohorts of a predetermined size and they progress through the program together. The program may also include summer internships in between academic years. Advantages of this program are the singular focus on your degree studies and the camaraderie that develops in these student cohorts. Disadvantages include the income reduction from leaving full-time employment and the relatively greater level of inexperience in professional positions (younger students on average).
Part-Time	While all programs provide applicants with an estimate of the time to degree completion (how many semesters/months/years it will take from start to finish), many also offer a part-time route that will take a longer period of time but will not require you to completely sacrifice your employment. Instead of taking three to five courses at a time during a semester, part-time programs may only demand that you take one or two courses in a semester. So a 2-year program becomes a 4-year program, which may be the only feasible approach for some individuals.

Professional	Some programs are geared toward working professionals. Courses are scheduled on evenings and Saturdays with greater emphasis placed on convenience. These may still be full-time programs with students taking three or four courses per semester. Advantages of professional programs include the scheduling convenience, time to degree, and greater peer learning shared from the pool of collective student experience (older students on average). Disadvantages consist of the workload and stress such programs can inflict on working professionals. Think about it—a 45- to 55-hour workweek plus 25 to 30 hours per week dedicated to the graduate program (9 hours of classroom time plus 18 hours of homework/study time).
Executive	These programs are less frequent but are becoming more popular because they bring in significant resources to universities. The programs tend to be pricey and there are stricter requirements for entering students. For example, they need to have 10 years or more of professional work experience and they need to hold positions in one of the two highest hierarchical levels in their organizations. Executives participating in these programs receive more premium services from the educational institutions.
Distance/Online	Research on the effectiveness of these virtual degrees is still inadequate. They are growing in popularity. Courses are conducted almost entirely via electronic means via the Internet and occasionally via videoconferencing. The degree is the same but you need to more thoroughly investigate the program's reputation and placement statistics of previous graduates. To view a full range of these distance programs, go to http://distance.gradschools.com and check out the options.

Admissions Requirements

Two main elements of this decision are (a) the requirements themselves; and (b) the application process and timeline. Let's consider the common admissions requirements first. One of the first items you have to deal with is taking any necessary qualifying exams. For any such exams you should find out the basic content areas covered on the exam, and when, where, and how the exam may be taken. Your performance on the qualifying exam can definitely enhance or inhibit your chances for acceptance into a graduate program. The better you do the more options you will have. Preparation is important. Back in the dinosaur days of the early 1990s when I prepared for the GMAT (the qualifying exam for MBA programs), I went out and bought a GMAT Test Prep book (a thick one as I recall).

The book went through the major content areas and reviewed key verbal and mathematical skills that would be covered in the exam. It also provided mock section exams and a full-blown mock exam. By the time I took the actual exam, I was ready and confident. Now you can prepare for these exams using either online or traditional hard-copy methods. These exams can usually be retaken if you perform poorly—for a small fee ($250 in the case of the GMAT).

The exam isn't the only requirement. There are usually GPA requirements and also either required or preferred work experience characteristics. Program requirements are easily found on the Web sites of universities providing graduate programs. The institutions typically provide a student profile that gives collective information about their admitted students (e.g., gender, race, average exam score, average GPA, years of work experience, average age).

Once you know the entrance requirements you need to look at the application process and deadlines. Because most qualifying exams cannot be taken anytime you want, it is imperative that you give yourself sufficient time to take the exam and have the scores sent to the universities to which you apply. Most, if not all, graduate programs also require official transcripts from an applicant's previous degree-granting institutions. They also usually demand a written statement of your accomplishments and/or your interest in earning that graduate degree. Finally, they expect letters of recommendation from professional references. The guidelines found in Chapter 6 related to professional references are equally applicable here.

TREK TASK 19

GRADUATE PROGRAM RESEARCH

Are you seriously considering earning a graduate degree? Check out any (or all) of the following Web sites for a plethora of graduate program information and related tips and articles.

www.gradschools.com
www.petersons.com/gradchannel/
www.mba.com

SUMMARY

The intent of this chapter and the previous one was to help you think through the various factors that will determine the relative strength of different career paths. It is not my role to dictate a path for you but rather to enable you to be more well-informed in how to research alternative paths and then choose for yourself. Refer back to the Person–Job Fit model (discussed in Chapter 1) as you acquire new information about the diverse paths you are considering. How well do the demands fit with your skills and passions? How well do the incentives or rewards of the paths fit with your career motives and aspirations? We have just about completed base camp. The next chapter will focus more on trends that are changing the careers landscape in general, and then you will be prepared to start climbing the mountain, pursuing whatever career routes that excite you the most.

TREK LIST

☐ **ENTREPRENEURIAL PATH**   Is it right for you?

1. Learn from the experiences of successful (and unsuccessful) entrepreneurs.
2. Discuss the implications of this path with those closest to you.
3. Test the fit with your Brand You message.
4. Create a skeleton business plan of your business idea.

☐ **GRADUATE SCHOOL**   I have identified my objectives for pursuing a graduate degree.

☐ **GRADUATE SCHOOL DECISIONS**   Consider the following factors:

1. *Timing.* When should I try to start a program?
2. *Degree type.* Do I want a masters or a doctorate? Why?
3. *Program institution.* What are the best institutions for my desired program? Costs/benefits trade-off?
4. *Program type.* Can I afford to go full-time? Will my current employer pay for the program?
5. *Admissions.* What are the requirements? When are applications due? Who can I talk to about the admissions criteria?

PART III

ASCENDING THE MOUNTAIN

. . . [O]n this morning the temperature was held in check by a biting wind that gusted down from the upper mountain, creating a windchill that dipped to perhaps forty below zero. . . . I continued climbing, and as I did so I grew colder and colder. The wind kicked up huge swirling waves of powder snow that washed down the mountain like breaking surf, plastering my clothing with frost. A carapace of ice formed over my goggles, making it difficult to see. I began to lose feeling in my feet. My fingers turned to wood. It seemed increasingly unsafe to keep going up in these conditions. I was at the head of the line, at 23,300 feet.

—*Jon Krakauer* (Into Thin Air, p. 161)

Climbing with oxygen for the first time in my life, I took a while to get used to it. Although the benefits of using gas at this altitude—24,000 feet—were genuine, they were hard to discern immediately. As I fought to catch my breath after moving past three climbers, the mask actually gave the illusion of asphyxiating me, so I tore it from my face—only to discover breathing was even harder without it.

—*Jon Krakauer* (Into Thin Air, p. 208)

I have never been 24,000 feet above sea level, nor have most human beings on this planet, except while in the pressurized cabins of commercial airplanes. The two chapter-opening quotes should give you a flavor of the challenges faced in ascending Everest. While base camp may have been challenging for you, we were nonetheless still at base camp, a relatively comfortable place. The hard work, at least for most of us, is searching for job leads and then successfully ascending through an organization's interview process to the point where we receive a job offer.

Think for a moment about job interviews you have had previously. Did you encounter any of the sensations that Krakauer described (albeit in less extreme forms)? Coldness, clammy hands, difficulty breathing? Consider yourself normal. Many of my students report similar anxieties while interviewing for jobs—and those were in mock interviews! As Charlotte told Wilber in the movie *Charlotte's Web,* "Chin up." You have been well prepared for this moment. You learned the three basic principles of a successful career—fit, passion, and a smile. You know yourself and what you want better than before the trek. You have strengthened your marketing materials (i.e., your résumé), and have developed a network of trusted individuals who want you to succeed. Finally, you have considered possible paths to arrive where you want to be. Now it is time to climb!

The chapters in this part of the trek will help you accomplish the following:

- Managing the job search process effectively by learning the steps of preparation, execution, and completion (Chapter 9)
- Preparing thoroughly for the interview process used by almost all organizations (Chapter 10)
- Conducting the interview itself in such a way that you outshine competing applicants (Chapter 11)
- Following up after the interview and then negotiating and evaluating the job offers that are extended to you (Chapter 12)

One final thought about the ascent. Krakauer likened it to an endurance race, not a thrill ride. It will take work and persistence, but it will be worth it later on. Oxygen masks ready? Let's climb.

Preparing for and Conducting an Effective Job Search

DILBERT: © Scott Adams/Dist. by United Feature Syndicate, Inc.

Never continue in a job you don't enjoy. If you're happy in what you're doing, you'll like yourself, you'll have inner peace. And if you have that, along with physical health, you will have had more success than you could possibly have imagined.

—*Johnny Carson*

The former king of late-night television, Johnny Carson, has provided us with the first guiding principle of conducting an effective job search—seek happiness and joy in your work. The man who held his job for 30 years became the best in the world at his line of work and was extremely successful in his career, although I will point out that some of that success came at the cost of a couple of failed marriages. Nevertheless, his quote is right on and prepares us for our ascent up Mount Career. This chapter and the next three chapters are intended to help you effectively land a job that you want (not a job you settle for, but one that you really feel good about).

The rest of this chapter will focus on three concepts:

- A framework to manage the job search process
- Sources for identifying tangible job leads
- Job application forms

MANAGING THE JOB SEARCH PROCESS

There are numerous reasons that people search for new jobs. Some of the most common catalysts for a job search are the following:

- Unemployment (victim of corporate layoffs, voluntary or involuntary exit)
- Graduation from a university degree program (and you want a job that better reflects your degree and its market value)
- Insufficient funds (financial expenses outstrip your income)
- Misfit (your current job is in a bad environment, you dread going to work and/or doing the tasks that your job requires)
- Midcareer transition (suffering from career burnout or your career path has hit a plateau)
- Greener grass (existing job is not bad, but you believe a better fit is possible elsewhere)
- Personal fulfillment (financial self-sufficiency allows you a very flexible choice)

Your rationale for conducting a job search has implications for the urgency of the search process and the sources of job leads you may use most frequently. For example, unemployment and dealing with insufficient funds involve a more intense search than the greener grass provocation. Regardless of the reason for your search, I will share with you what I believe are the key steps in preparing for and conducting an effective job search. Managing this process can be a full-time job and should be approached in an organized, comprehensive manner. The three parts to an effective job search management process are preparation, execution, and completion.

PREPARATION

1. Define the scope of your search.
2. Identify potential employers.
3. Research, research, research.
4. Update your "passport" (résumé and cover letter, plus portfolio documents).
5. Develop a tracking tool.

EXECUTION

6. Tap your network members first.
7. Tap other sources of job leads.

8. Audition effectively in the hiring process.

9. Never burn bridges and always follow up in a timely, professional manner.

COMPLETION

10. Negotiate the job offer.

11. Audit the process (whether it ended successfully or not).

12. Persist without discouragement

These 12 steps will help you ascend the mountain and obtain a job you desire. Of course, step 10 will not always be a part of the process. Almost all job searchers experience failure and rejection at some point, so step 12 is important throughout the process.

Preparation

Preparation precedes power, and you want power in your job search. The five steps described in detail in the following paragraphs will help you remain focused and organized throughout the search process. Such an approach will increase your likelihood of a successful search.

Define the Scope. If you view the job search as a project that will have an end (I certainly do), then one rule of effective project management certainly applies to the search process. Perhaps the most important factor of project success is thorough, accurate definition of the project's scope. Project scope includes the purpose of the project, key success indicators, and the desired time frame and budgeted resources. Applied to the job search, it means that you decide upon your search objective, key criteria you want to satisfy, and the desired time frame for completion of the job search. Let's examine these three components of the scope more closely.

In *Alice's Adventures in Wonderland,* Alice is lost in the woods and encounters the Cheshire Cat. Alice asks Cheshire Cat which of the different paths she should take. He responds, "That depends a great deal on where you want to go." Alice then says, "I don't much care where—," to which Cheshire Cat responds, "Then it doesn't matter which way you go."[1] The point is that if you don't know what your search objective is, your search is meaningless. So what is it that you want? What is your quest? (If you have seen Monty Python's *Holy Grail* film, you can start quoting the movie here. One approach I recommend is to answer the question: Where do you want to be professionally in three years? If you can answer that, then work backwards, identifying intermediate steps that help you arrive at that destination.

The next component is key criteria. At the start of your job search, many paths can be traveled. Numerous potential jobs will fulfill some of your criteria, but which jobs satisfy your most important criteria? What is the most important factor you are trying to satisfy with a new job? It could be challenging work, flexible scheduling, positive work environment, shorter commute, location, income level, or any number of other factors. The important thing to do here is to clearly identify your most important criteria; those criteria you will not compromise in your job search.

---

[1] Carroll, L. S. *Alice's Adventures in Wonderland.*

Finally, what is your time frame for completion? It may be yesterday (extreme urgency) or it may be several months from now. The answer to this question depends on your current financial status, needs of dependents, your own sanity, level of burnout, severance packages or other income sources, and other factors related to your urgency to have a new job.

Those are the three components related to defining the scope of your job search. Now it is your turn to apply this first crucial step of the job-search management process.

 TREK TASK 20

JOB SEARCH SCOPE

Define the scope of your job search at this point in time. Write down your search objective. Identify three to five key criteria that need to be met by the job you obtain. Rank those criteria in order of importance. Determine the desired time frame for completion of your job search.

Identify Potential Employers. Based upon your job search scope, particularly the key criteria, you now need to determine the potential employers that can satisfy those criteria. I am not a big advocate for a scattered search process where the job seeker sends out 100 resumes to a broad group of employers. I like Pepper de Callier's approach of narrowing your possible companies to 10. However, take it a step further and concentrate on five to seven of those companies as your preferred targets. If you are not constrained greatly by location or industry, I suggest that you strive for companies that are admired in their industries and have the reputation for being great places to work. *Fortune* magazine enables us to find such companies in the United States more easily with its annual issues, "The 100 Best Companies to Work For in America" (comes out in early January) and "The Most Admired U.S. Companies" (comes out in March). All other factors being equal, go with companies with strong reputations and a track record of spending significant resources on development of employees. Identification of potential employers and the next step (research) are closely intertwined. You will need to conduct substantial research to identify organizations of interest and then, after you have targeted those organizations, guess what? Conduct more specific research!

Research, Research, Research. Chapter 7 offered many suggestions for researching possible paths. Just make sure that you don't take any shortcuts with this step. When I was finishing my Ph.D. and going through my search process, I obtained roughly 20 manila file folders and labeled one per university to which I applied. All my research about that position and institution was then compiled into that folder. One of our main problems when doing Internet research is that we find information on the Internet but don't save that information, either in highlighted or comprehensive form. *Conducting an effective job search can be a full-time job (or at least a rigorous part-time job), so put in the time if you truly want to climb.*

Update Your Passport. The main content of your résumé and cover letter will need to be revisited, especially if you have spent significant time in your current organization without updating your résumé. Make sure that your contact information is current and that your résumé objective reflects the scope of your search. Revise any additional educational or work experience items that have occurred since your last résumé update. Most importantly, incorporate significant accomplishments and skills that are not yet on your résumé. I make it a point to update my résumé monthly with any accomplishments or recently developed skills or certifications; this way I don't forget many important results. Keep in mind that you will further tailor your résumé and cover letter in the Execution phase when you formally apply for different positions.

Develop a Tracking Tool. I mentioned that I used manila folders to keep materials about each position in one of my most recent job searches. I also created an Excel spreadsheet to track the status of the various positions for which I had applied. The spreadsheet contained fields for the name and contact information of the main organizational contact. It also contained fields for indicating whether or not I had sent my résumé and additional application materials. Keep track of any critical information that you want to organize for your search. You could incorporate your key criteria into the spreadsheet to see how well different jobs meet your criteria. It can also serve as a checklist to ensure that you have taken all of the necessary steps in the typical hiring process.

Execution

Even the most prepared mountain climber may meet an untimely demise if he fails to execute properly on his ascent up the mountain. Carelessness, faulty equipment, and faulty assumptions can all lead to accidents on the path to the summit. All of your research and organization should make you feel more confident and optimistic about a successful job search, but you still need to package yourself on paper and in person to secure the job you want. The Execution stage is about generating job leads and selling yourself to prospective employers in order to receive job offers.

Tap Your Network. The first two steps of the Execution stage are designed to generate job leads that meet your key criteria and search objective. From your research in the Preparation stage, you should have identified some potential employers and/or positions that best meet your criteria. Now you need to secure the leads and land some interviews. Your network should be the first and primary source that you turn to for those leads. Your first activity should be to alert your network members that you are searching for a job and disclose to them your search objective (in other words, err on the side of being more specific). Second, you may want to send your updated résumé to your closest network members and ask them for feedback. This gets your résumé out in front of others and allows you to draw upon the wisdom of others. Third, ask them for referrals to any persons they know who are employees of your target employers. The odds that you obtain an interview with an organization increase considerably when you have been referred by a trusted professional who knows a decision maker in that organization. Finally, keep your network members updated on your search progress and be optimistic and persistent.

Tap Other Sources of Job Leads. While networking is the best source of job leads, if your network members cannot provide you with leads for all the jobs you want to apply for, then you need to turn to other sources. The following table lists numerous sources with some comments about what benefits they may provide.

SOURCE	DESCRIPTION OR COMMENTS
Employers	Once you identify prospective employers that appeal to you, direct contacts with those employers can be an effective entrée into their organizations. Requesting informational interviews, researching the employer's Web site, and trying to create a position tailored to your strengths can result in a job lead.
College career placement services	For those of you completing a university degree, you should get to know your institution's career services. These organizations usually provide free career services to students and discounted services to alumni. Services usually range from résumé critiquing to promoting job fairs to bringing companies on campus for hiring graduating students.
Internet	Prominent job Web sites such as www.monster.com, www.hotjobs.com, and www.careerbuilder.com offer numerous job leads although applying for them online has not shown to be all that effective (less than 10%, according to Bolles). The Internet is fantastic for researching the employers and looking at job descriptions to get a better feel for what employers are looking for.
Professional associations	Most professions have national and regional associations that are excellent sources of professional trends and, to a certain extent, job openings. It is important to learn which association is the most credible and well-connected from a networking standpoint.
Employment directories	Printed directories of regional and local employers are usually available through public and university libraries; online directories are also available for major cities and metropolitan areas.
Want ads	Not the best source of professional jobs but can be beneficial for showing salary ranges and required qualifications for some positions. Be careful with ads that point you to an anonymous P.O. box address but do not announce the company—some are legit, others are not.

Employment agencies	Employment agencies come in various shapes (private and public) and sizes. Private agencies usually charge job seekers a fee payable upon their offer of a permanent job. Assess the agency's reputation, costs and financial arrangement, expertise in your career objective, and scope of services provided. Public agencies don't usually charge a fee for their services, which usually are more informational than actually securing you a position with a company.
Career/job fairs	These are often held on college campuses and in high-traffic business areas in cities. Check with your institution for a calendar of such activities. Also, local newspapers and business publications generally promote these events to their communities. Dress professionally and take business cards and résumé copies. Think about your elevator pitch, which you will use to introduce yourself to employers. If you can obtain an advanced listing of participating employers, target 8 to 10 that you most want to contact and conduct some research on them.
Chambers of commerce	If location and commute time are important criteria, then the chamber of commerce in your desired location can be very helpful. Chambers have information on local employers (company size, reputation, and growth trends). They can also help you personally meet with local company executives.
Internships/volunteering	Either paid or unpaid internships help you get your foot in the door and may pave the way for a permanent position. They are attractive for employers, allowing both you and the employer a test drive to see if the fit is right. Voluntary activities can enhance your résumé, build your network, and hone valuable skills and experience.

 TREK TASK 21
SOURCES OF JOB LEADS

Now go back and review these sources carefully. Place a checkmark next to those sources that you think will be most beneficial and that you plan to use in your search. Identify one action step you need to take to start tapping that source for actual job leads.

Audition Effectively in the Hiring Process. From your first interaction with a prospective employer until you accept that employer's job offer, consider yourself an actor on stage going through an intense audition. Members of the employing organization comprise your audience. You need to send them away wanting an encore: They should want further interaction with you! Your audition starts with how you look on paper (e.g., résumé, cover letter, and job application forms). It ends with one or multiple interviews with company decision makers and the acceptance of an offer. The next three chapters address principles of an effective "audition" related to the interviewing process, and the subsequent follow-up activities that are overlooked by so many job seekers.

Never Burn Bridges and Always Follow Up. Chapter 12 will specifically describe important follow-up steps that you should take during the hiring process. Let me just stress one more time that you are always on stage during this process. So act professionally at all times and never, *never* burn a bridge with a prospective employer. Even if you are rejected by that organization, they will remember how you conducted yourself, and this can enhance or inhibit your future opportunities with that organization (and potentially with other organizations).

Completion

The aim of any job seeker is that by following the Execution stage to receive one, or better yet, multiple job offers to consider. If your Execution stage produces positive results, the Completion stage closes the deal. If the results of your execution weren't so favorable then the Completion stage focuses on learning from failure and dealing effectively with discouragement.

Negotiate the Job Offer. Chapter 12 will offer insights on how to negotiate job offers. You need to consider how badly you want the position, your status in the hiring processes for other positions, which aspects of the offer are negotiable, and how well the offer fits your predetermined search criteria. Effective negotiation skills are important to many organizational roles, so this is an important skill set to learn from the outset of your career. One challenge in this step is to determine our true value to the organization. It is common for job seekers to underestimate their potential worth to an organization. Less common but not less problematic is the job seeker who overestimates his value. You don't receive an offer unless the company wants you. Keep that in mind and I'll share some specific tips in Chapter 12.

Audit the Process. Whether or not you receive an offer for a position, after the final outcome you should conduct a candid audit on why you did or did not get the job. Assess the effectiveness of your written documents (résumé and cover letter). Did you get an interview? If you are consistently being passed over for initial interviews then one of two things is likely happening: (a) your résumé is ineffective, in either appearance or content; or (b) you are applying for positions for which you are not qualified. If you are conducting many first interviews but not moving beyond that point, then you should reevaluate your interviewing skills. For jobs or employers that you really want, it is certainly okay to ask for some feedback if you don't receive an offer. This information may help you if you apply again to that company in the future.

Persist without Discouragement. I know about this firsthand. Two years ago, after several months of upheaval in the work environment of the College of Business, I was ready to go elsewhere. I applied to several different universities and had initial interviews with many of them at our annual management conference in Denver. From my research I determined that there were four positions that I felt offered the best professional and personal fit. I received on-campus interviews from those institutions. When you are unsuccessful in a hiring situation, it is natural to have some doubts about your preparation, marketable skills, and interviewing capabilities. You need to maintain the belief that eventually you will successfully find a job that fits you well. It certainly can be discouraging, but you can't let the despair overwhelm you. Remember that employers want evidence of a positive attitude—and discouragement comes through clearly in job interviews. Tough as it may be, *stay positive!*

JOB APPLICATION GUIDELINES

We need to share one more concept about the job search process. After you have generated job leads and made contact (either physically or virtually) with those employers, many of them will require you to complete a formal job application form. Don't overlook the importance of these forms. Levitt offers the following valuable tips for successfully completing job application forms.[2]

- Read and follow the directions. Prepare each section slowly and carefully.
- Make your application neat, with legible handwriting or correct data entry—no smudges or rumpled edges.
- Use the correct lines or spaces for your answers.
- Practice on a copy of the application, squeeze in as much positive information about yourself as possible, and abbreviate to fit information in the spaces provided.
- Answer every question. Use N/A (not applicable) if the question does not pertain to you. This shows that you did not overlook the question or skip it purposely.
- Use perfect spelling, grammar, and punctuation. Use specialized terminology correctly. (You never get a second chance to make a good first impression!)
- Include a second telephone number of a person who is readily available and willing to take messages for you. You can't afford to miss calls from employers!
- Make certain all information is accurate (dates, addresses, telephone and fax numbers, names—*everything*).
- Be honest. Employers check the facts and immediately eliminate any candidate who has supplied false information.
- Date and sign the application. Some organizations invalidate an application if it is not signed and dated!

---

[2] Levitt, J. G. (2000). *Your career: How to make it happen.* Belmont, CA: South-Western Educational Publishing, p. 173.

This chapter has suggested an overall framework to conduct an effective job search through the Preparation, Execution, and Completion stages and offered guidelines for completing job application forms. The next two chapters describe the most nerve-wracking yet invigorating steps in the Execution stage of the job search—preparing for and shining in the job interview. The job interview is usually the abyss that separates exceptional candidates from good candidates. Looking good on paper is one thing; wowing people in person is something altogether different.

▲🚶🚶 TREK LIST

☐ **JOB SEARCH MANAGEMENT PROCESS**   I know the three main phases of an effective process: preparation, execution, and completion.

☐ **SCOPE**   I have determined the scope and key criteria for my job search.

☐ **FINDING JOB LEADS**   I have talked with my network members and used other sources to obtain leads for the jobs I want.

☐ **CHIN UP**   I know that rejection is a normal part of the job search process and I will not become discouraged if I don't get what I want immediately.

☐ **JOB APPLICATIONS**   I have learned key guidelines for completing application forms.

Preparing for the Interview

10

Not knowing enough about the company or position, displaying a bad attitude or inquiring about compensation prematurely can all leave a negative impression with hiring managers. For job seekers, the interview represents a time to shine. Thorough preparation—including researching the employer, rehearsing responses to common questions and understanding appropriate topics to discuss—is the key to avoiding potential pitfalls.

—*Max Messner, CEO of Robert Half International and author of* Job Hunting for Dummies

In most cases, job seekers (especially soon-to-be college graduates) are not initially approached by prospective employers with offers for employment. We have to go out and work very hard to showcase our abilities to those employers. I want to emphasize two phrases from Messner's quote. First, "the interview represents a time to shine." Think of yourself as being on stage, because you are. As with most performing artists, how well you perform on that stage is predicated on your level of preparation while off the stage. The second point is **"Thorough preparation . . . is the key to avoiding potential pitfalls."**

Paths that ascend strenuous mountain terrain often cross several dangerous spots, such as patches of ice or a deep, menacing abyss. These challenging areas of the path raise adrenaline and anxiety, causing fear and trepidation but also exhilaration and clarity of focus. The climbers who successfully cross the abyss are those who are best prepared and who concentrate their abilities most effectively on solely executing the task at hand. They are not thinking about the summit or future difficulties on their path. They are completely focused and they execute their plan meticulously. The job interview, especially for less-experienced applicants, can be likened to an abyss on our career mountain. This chapter provides a model with specific steps to help you prepare for the interview. Chapter 11 describes how to execute effectively during the course of the interview itself.

INTERVIEW PREPARATION MODEL

As with most aspects of career management, preparation is critical to the success of a job interview. I developed the model shown in Figure 10.1 to emphasize four main categories of preparatory steps that applicants should follow before a scheduled interview. As you may have guessed, the four steps follow a mountain climbing theme. Once you have decided upon a route (or at least have a route opened up to you by receiving an invitation for an initial interview), the first step is to *know your route.* Learn as much as you can about this possible path before you discuss it in an interview setting. Second, *visualize the ascent.* This means to practice, or rehearse, what might happen during the interview. It also means using mental imagery to view yourself successfully performing in the interview (crossing the abyss victoriously). Third, when you leave base camp and head up the mountain, the climate becomes colder, more inconsistent, and with gustier winds, so climbers must *dress appropriately.* Finally, you must *stack your pack,* meaning that you take with you helpful materials which may be requested during the interviewing process.

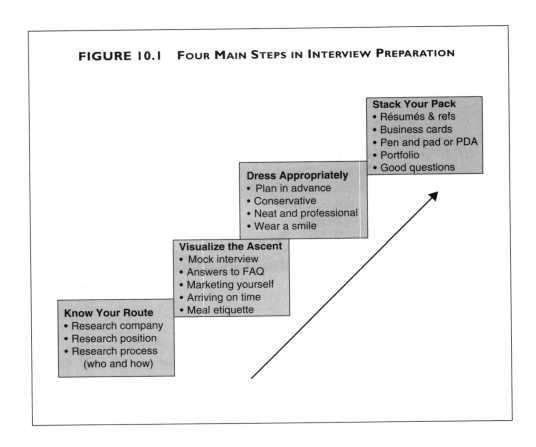

FIGURE 10.1   FOUR MAIN STEPS IN INTERVIEW PREPARATION

Stack Your Pack
- Résumés & refs
- Business cards
- Pen and pad or PDA
- Portfolio
- Good questions

Dress Appropriately
- Plan in advance
- Conservative
- Neat and professional
- Wear a smile

Visualize the Ascent
- Mock interview
- Answers to FAQ
- Marketing yourself
- Arriving on time
- Meal etiquette

Know Your Route
- Research company
- Research position
- Research process
  (who and how)

The model demonstrates my belief that there is some order in this preparation, starting with painstaking research and ending with you leaving for the interview in appropriate attire and prepared with the right items to help you cross the abyss. Let's examine each preparation category in detail.

Know Your Route

It may seem to you as if my continual harping on the value of thorough research is like beating a dead horse. However, because time is a scarce commodity for most job seekers, you may be surprised how often applicants skip this crucial step, particularly when they already possess some experience in the occupation or industry for which they are applying. Chapter 7 touched upon numerous areas of research that you should conduct of a more general nature as you are considering possible career paths. However, now that you have an interview with an organization, you need to take the research to a more detailed level. The three components of your route that need to be more thoroughly researched to enhance your interview preparation are the company, the position, and the interviewing process. Here is what you need to know and why:

- *Company.* At the bare minimum, you should know the major facts about the company (main products and services, geographical scope of activities, CEO, stock price if publicly traded, key competitors, and position within the company's industry). The more you can learn in advance about the company's culture, unique training programs and employee benefits, key financials, and strategic objectives, the better chance you have at dazzling your interviewer with your effort to learn the company's business and with the depth of the questions you will ask in the interview.

- *Position.* Obtaining additional information beyond the formal job description may be difficult, but you want to review carefully the required and preferred qualifications identified in the job description. If there is no formal job description (a rare occurrence for professional positions) then make sure you understand the key expectations and priorities for whoever would be hired in the position. Remember that the company will not have invited you for an interview unless they think you are at least moderately qualified for the position (or else they are *really* desperate!). But look at the skills they want to be used in the position and expect that you will be asked some behavioral-based interview questions that probe your past demonstration of those skills. Finally, if you realize that you fail to meet a couple of the position requirements, be prepared to discuss how you will overcome that deficiency.

- *Process.* If the person who invites you for the interview doesn't proactively give you this information, then you need to ask about the steps in the hiring process. Companies use myriad interviewing and testing activities in an attempt to hire the right people. At the very least, you want to know about the nature of the initial interview you will have with the company. Who will be conducting the interview? Is it someone in HR? A hiring manager? A senior executive (for smaller organizations)? Will it be one-on-one, or with multiple employees? Where will the interview take place? Some organizations will even send applicants who reach the interview stage of the hiring process a packet of informational materials about their organizations.

The bottom line with this Research stage is that you want your preparation and organizational knowledge to enable you to stand out from other applicants who didn't take the time for this stage.

TREK TASK 22

COMPANY RESEARCH

Pick a company you are interested in and research its Web site and other relevant information you can find on the Internet. Develop three to five strong questions you would want to ask an interviewer from that company.

Visualize the Ascent

Steve Scott, holder of the U.S. record in the mile run and currently the track coach at Cal State San Marcos, described how he would mentally run the race *before* he physically ran the race. This visualization process, also known as mental imagery, is used by numerous world-class performers in diverse professions. When faced with a stressful performance (such as an interview), mentally rehearsing the delivery and content of the performance can be very beneficial. Among the following are several activities that you can do to prepare mentally for a successful interview.

- *Mock interview.* There is nothing quite so revealing (and perhaps painful) as watching your performance on videotape. So I urge you to conduct a mock interview. Find out if your campus career or placement center provides such a service for students. If not, ask a close member of your network if he or she could help you out. If at all possible, videotape the interview so that you and/or others can evaluate your performance. You will find an example of an interview evaluation form that I use with my students at the end of this chapter. Remember that the mock interview is a special type of role play, and as with all role plays, you will derive greater value if you really get into the role. Dress the part, use an actual job description, think about specific questions you would ask, visualize the real interview.

- *Answers to frequently asked questions.* Mentally rehearse or even write down effective answers to common interview questions. You can expect certain questions in most initial interviews, such as What are your weaknesses? Why do you want to work with our company? Where do you see yourself in the next three years? and the old interview standby icebreaker statement, Tell me about yourself. In the next chapter, we will discuss strategies for answering these and other common interview questions. The important point for now is that you should think through possible questions that you may be faced with in the interview and consider how you will respond.

- *Marketing message.* The interview is another opportunity for you to sell what you can offer to a prospective employer. What message do you want the interviewer to take away from those few precious minutes you spend together? I usually prepare for interviews by identifying the two or three qualities that I can contribute to the organization, and that I believe will be most attractive to the organization for the position for which I have applied. Then I visualize how I might be able to emphasize those qualities during the interview by citing specific accomplishments, saying particular words or phrases, and sharing memorable (but brief) stories. Remember Brand You?! Now is the time to consider how you can best communicate your unique brand message.

- *On-time arrival.* Do you know how to reach your interview location? You *never* want to be late for your interview. Visualize the route you expect to take and, if necessary, ask the company for any special directions related to parking and arrival at the interview location. How early should you plan to arrive for an interview? Most experts suggest 5 to 10 minutes but no earlier than 15 minutes, because that can disrupt the normal flow of work activity at the company. If your interview takes place in a high-traffic area, give yourself plenty of time. I suggest arriving at the company's parking lot 15 to 30 minutes in advance and then use the extra time in your car to mentally prepare for the interview.

- *Meal etiquette.* This activity will not be relevant for every interview situation, but if a lunch or dinner is part of your interview process then you must not forget that the meal *is* part of the interview. You are still onstage and a common flaw of applicants is to let their guard down somewhat during the meal. They may become overly casual, unprofessional, or at the extreme, slightly intoxicated. I will not give you an extensive list of etiquette principles. However, here are a couple of important principles: follow your hosts' lead in ordering, and don't order messy foods (e.g., ribs, crab or lobster, etc.) or foods with which you are not familiar. Focus more on the conversation with your hosts than on the food.

Visualize yourself confidently and effectively conducting your interview. Think about how you want the interview conversation to unfold. The interview is a sales pitch and an audition for future performances with that company. Imagine how you will feel when the company makes you an offer and subsequently, how you will feel on your first day on the job. Then go to work to make that image a reality.

▲🚶🚶   **TREK TASK 23**
MOCK INTERVIEW

Conduct a mock interview. Dress in professional interview attire, bring a current résumé and an actual job description. If possible, videotape the interview. Review and evaluate the interview. Ask the interviewer or someone else from your network to provide an additional evaluation of your interview.

Dress Appropriately

According to previous research, the factor that has the second greatest impact on interview effectiveness (from the interviewer's perspective) is the applicant's image and appearance.[1] Much of that image and appearance is how you dress along with the whole aura of professionalism you bring. In the interview, you are trying to sell a product to the employer—the product is *you*! Your physical appearance is the product's packaging.

Plan your interview attire in advance. If you plan to be involved in several interviews (such as when you are close to graduation and seeking a full-time position), then you should invest in a couple of conservative interview suits. Find out what the company's dress standards are and then dress at least a step above that for the interview. Pick your best colors and get plenty of sleep the night before the interview.

In general, conservative attire is the way to go for your interview. Here are some specific guidelines:

- No flashy-colored suits (if you glow in the dark, that's too flashy!).
- Conservative hairstyles (none of your attire should distract the interviewer from what you will say during the interview).
- For women, avoid multiple and large dangling earrings.
- For both men and women, remove any body rings (from nose, navel, tongue, etc.).
- Avoid excessive jewelry.
- For men, wear fashionable but not novelty ties (nothing that lights up, plays music, or has cartoon characters).

Your appearance should be neat and professional—shirts should be clean and pressed, any facial hair should be trimmed and neatly combed. Shoes should be polished. Socks should match. No runs in the pantyhose. Anything you bring with you to the interview—such as an attaché case, purse, or your portfolio—should look orderly and professional.

---

[1] Levitt, J. G. (2000). *Your career: How to make it happen.* Belmont, CA: South-Western Educational Publishing, p. 198.

The most important accessory that you need in order to complete your professional ensemble is your smile. Remember that employers won't hire many people they do not like. Enjoy yourself, and share your smile. Employers look for passion in applicants. Your smile demonstrates your enthusiasm, and if you can smile in a stressful interview then you can smile during those stressful times on the job. By the way, since you will be smiling, make sure you don't have any particles stuck in those teeth, and remember the comment of Eddie Murphy's character from the movie *Shrek,* "Do I detect a hint of minty freshness?" Fresh breath is a must. If you smoke, don't do it right before the interview.

These are the basics about dressing appropriately for professional interviews: plan what you'll wear, stay conservative, look neat and professional, and smile genuinely during the interview. Why is this so important? People tend to form perceptions very quickly when they first meet a new individual; it is called primacy effect. Furthermore, people tend to infer an applicant's unobservable traits based upon a single physical characteristic; this is referred to as halo effect. So manage those first and subsequent impressions of the interviewer by presenting a professional image.

Stack Your Pack

As you go to your interview, make sure that you have the following materials with you:

- *Career portfolio.* Most, if not all, of the remaining items can be carried in your portfolio. (*Note:* your portfolio binder should look neat and professional; I have had students turn in their portfolios for their class assignment in used binders which they used to save a couple of bucks. Remember that everything about you projects an image when you are on the interview stage!)

- *Extra résumé copies.* You can store extra résumés in plastic protector pages in the portfolio or in the back pocket of the portfolio binder; you can never predict who may want (or need) to see your résumé when you are interviewed.

- *References.* The company may have asked for some professional references before your initial interview but, if not, you can bet that they will at the end of the interview if they still see you as a viable candidate for the position. Have several copies of your one-page references document with you so that you can produce one for employers upon demand.

- *Business cards.* It is always good to have a supply of business cards available, more for networking while interviewing than for the actual interviewing process itself. Be careful about using company business cards if your current employer doesn't know you are looking elsewhere.

- *Pen and paper (or PDA).* Should you take notes during an interview? For the majority of the interview time, I would suggest that you avoid taking notes—it makes it more difficult to carry on a meaningful two-way conversation; however, when the interviewer asks if you have any questions for her, then it is not inappropriate to say something like this: "Yes, I do have a few that I wrote down as I was doing some research on your company" and take out your pad of paper (or even a sheet of paper will do). Then you may jot down some notes to those specific questions. If you are a PDA guru, then whip out your Palm Pilot and use that to note the highlights of the interviewer's responses to your questions.

- *Three to five good questions.* Remember that the interview is also an opportunity for you to assess the company, so be prepared to ask meaningful questions. As described in the previous bulleted item, prepare some questions in advance. When asked if you have any questions, never say no or "none that I can think of." I have had several recruiters and hiring managers tell me that the questions applicants ask are as big a factor in interview success as the responses applicants provide to the interviewers' questions. Questions should focus more on the company and how you can benefit the company, not how the company will benefit you—you don't want to come across in a self-serving manner.

 TREK TASK 24

INTERVIEW READINESS CHECK

Double-check your portfolio! Do you have all of the items you need? At the very least, you should have extra résumé copies and questions you want to ask in the interview.

Having read this chapter you should be much better prepared for any interview. However, you can be well-prepared and still mess up the execution of the interview itself. The next chapter offers ideas for winning the interview battle.

TREK LIST

- ☐ **INTERVIEW PREPARATION MODEL**   I have committed this model to *memory*. Interview preparation is so critical—remember the four steps (research, visualize, dress, pack).

- ☐ **RESEARCH**   I have spent sufficient time learning about the organization with which I am interviewing.

- ☐ **VISUALIZE**   I have practiced my interviewing skills via a mock interview and/or mentally rehearsing my responses to common interview questions.

- ☐ **ON TIME**   I know how to get to the interview and will give myself enough time to arrive there 5 to 10 minutes earlier than the interview time.

- ☐ **DRESS**   My attire and appearance are professional and appropriate for the interview.

- ☐ **PACK**   I have extra résumé copies, business cards, references page, and a pad of paper for notes and questions.

MOCK INTERVIEW EVALUATION FORM

Evaluation Criteria

For each checklist item, please indicate how well you demonstrated that interview skill—NI = needs improvement, S = satisfactory, O = outstanding. Please provide appropriate detailed comments (especially for any S or NI items).

Checklist Item	NI / S / O	Comments
Attitude		
Projected confidence but not arrogance	NI S O	
Projected enthusiasm	NI S O	
Demonstrated knowledge of and interest in the employer	NI S O	
Came across as being likable	NI S O	
Image and appearance		
Dressed conservatively and neatly	NI S O	
Made effort to be groomed properly	NI S O	
Looked alert and attentive	NI S O	
Appeared comfortable and calm	NI S O	
Verbal Communication		
Projected a pleasant tone of voice	NI S O	
Avoided filler words (e.g., um, uh, you know)	NI S O	
Avoided credibility robbers	NI S O	
Used positive words and phrases	NI S O	
Used correct grammar	NI S O	
Remained focused (no rambling)	NI S O	
Demonstrated sense of humor	NI S O	
Provided knowledgeable responses	NI S O	
Asked quality questions	NI S O	
Demonstrated research of the company	NI S O	
Used SAR stories appropriately	NI S O	
Nonverbal Communication		
Smiled sufficiently	NI S O	
Made effective eye contact	NI S O	
Used hand gestures (without fidgeting)	NI S O	
Projected pleasant facial expressions	NI S O	
Maintained good posture	NI S O	
Avoided distracting mannerisms	NI S O	
Avoided the appearance of nervousness	NI S O	

General Comments

Shining in the Interview

> [T]he balance of power has shifted. It's no longer up to the company to sell you on the job; it's up to you to sell yourself to the company. In fact, it wouldn't hurt to be a little—dare we say it—humble.[1]
>
> —*Stacey Bradford*

Stacey Bradford, author of the book *Ace That Interview,* has effectively captured some fundamental truths about the interview process today. Several years ago, at the height of the dot-com craze, applicants had the upper hand. Companies were offering signing bonuses, significant stock options, and above-market salaries. The labor talent pool was shallow and companies were growing rapidly in the red-hot economy. Times have changed! The labor pool is much deeper because of the experienced ex-employees of companies that used layoffs to deal with the souring economy. While job creation is not terrible by any stretch, the reality is that competition for existing job openings is fierce and employers have the upper hand right now. So humility, gratitude, professionalism, and an effective sales presentation (because an interview is a sales presentation) is necessary now more than ever before.

To succeed at interviewing requires considerable courage. I recently heard an insightful quote about courage attributed to an anonymous author: "Courage is not the absence of fear. It is the mastery of fear." You will have some butterflies, some fear, related to any interview for a position you actually care about. The trick is to harness that fear and make it work for you—and that embodies courage. It also takes experience and a mastery of four essential interviewing components.

Your ability to shine in the interview process will depend upon your ability to manage each of the following aspects of the interview:

- The interviewer's first impressions
- The conversation (answering and asking questions effectively)
- Your BE-attitudes
- Closing the interview

---

[1] Bradford, S. *Ace that interview.* Smart Money.com.

FIRST IMPRESSIONS

A widely researched concept called *primacy effect* suggests that we make lasting perceptions of others based on minimal observations and information captured in the first few minutes of our interactions with those persons. In fact, careers author Julie Levitt asserts, "When first meeting, people often form opinions about others within 30 seconds or less. . . . This first 30 seconds can make or break an interview."[2] She led a research effort that asked the following question of interviewers: "What influences interviewers to perceive applicants positively during interviews?"[3] Interviewers reported *four main applicant factors* that caused the most impact on interview perceptions: *attitude* (40% impact), *image and appearance* (25%), *verbal and nonverbal communication* (25%), and actual *job qualifications* (10%). Keep in mind that you are not likely to be invited to an interview unless the employer believes you are at least somewhat qualified for the position. So it isn't surprising that job qualifications would be less of a factor in interview success. First impressions will largely be focused on the image/appearance characteristics of attire and physical appearance (which was discussed in the previous chapter). However, some other early impressions will be made based upon the following:

- *Interaction with receptionist/secretary.* In fact, many companies make the receptionist an undeclared member of the hiring team. Applicants who treat receptionists or secretaries with disdain, or in a demeaning manner, eliminate themselves from further consideration. These interactions signal something about the applicant's attitude—don't overlook them!

- *Handshake.* Be firm, neither limp (no finger shakes) nor crushing (no bruised bones).

- *Initial communication signals.* Does your voice convey nervousness? Do your words convey arrogance? Can you make effective eye contact with the interviewer? Are you slouching in your chair? These early signals tell the interviewer a great deal about your confidence, comfort level, and overall professionalism and communication skills.

Think about what first impressions you want to generate with your interviewer. At the very least, you want to be viewed as professional, enthusiastic, and likable (that's why employers will hire you!).

 TREK TASK 25

INTERVIEW FIRST IMPRESSIONS

Review your mock interview. Look at the first 2 minutes of the interview. What signals did you send the interviewer? Better yet, ask someone else to review the interview and give their impressions.

---

[2] Levitt, J. G. (2000). *Your career: How to make it happen.* Belmont, CA: South-Western Educational Publishing, p. 198.

[3] Ibid., p. 198 (see Levitt's Chapter 11 for further details).

MANAGING AN EFFECTIVE CONVERSATION

Let's assume you have made a positive initial impression on the interview. Your next step is to manage the conversation effectively between you and the interviewer. This requires practice and skill in both what you say (verbal communication) and how you say it (nonverbal communication). First, let me share a few nonverbal tips with you. Then I will discuss verbal communication issues and go over frequently asked questions along with some strategies for effectively responding to those questions.

Nonverbal Communication Tips

If you look at the interview evaluation form at the end of the last chapter, you will see seven items related to nonverbal communication. The items are repeated here but placed in a slightly different order to represent three general categories: likability, professionalism, and nervous distractions. For each item I offer comments about what the tip means and why it is important.

LIKABILITY

Smile sufficiently

Smiles break the tension and make both parties feel more comfortable; and no, you don't need a Barbie-doll-permanent smile to be effective.

Project pleasant facial expressions

I have seen many mock interviews and conducted several real interviews where the applicants looked like they were patients sitting in a chair at the dentist's office, the impending pain evident on their faces. You should look like you are actually enjoying the experience.

PROFESSIONALISM

Make effective eye contact

Do not engage in a staring contest, but our society perceives eye contact as a manifestation of integrity and confidence.

Maintain good posture

You remember when your mother said "Sit up straight"? Even if you live in a laid-back culture such as Southern California, slouching in the interview chair is a ticket to leave the interview chair.

NERVOUS DISTRACTIONS

Avoid the appearance of nervousness

There are countless ways that our inner nervousness can be manifested to the outside world (e.g., sweaty palms or brows, chewing fingernails, etc.). Knowledge of any nervous habits is the first step in eliminating them in the formal interview setting.

Avoid distracting mannerisms

Look at your mock interview tape. Do you observe any distracting habits? They can involve hair twisting, tapping fingers on a table, or just about any other behavior that redirects the interviewer's attention away from what you say to what you are doing.

Use effective hand gestures (no fidgeting)

Many of us don't use our hands enough to communicate effectively. To a lesser extent, some of us overcommunicate with our hands, gesturing wildly and too frequently. If your hands never leave your lap, that is a problem. Watch out for the dreaded desk-tapping of nervous fingers, or the clicking of a ball-point pen. Hand gestures should accentuate your message rather than annoy the interviewer.

A couple of final thoughts about nonverbal communication. First, never yawn during an interview! This is impolite and it tells the interviewer that you are either bored or tired. So make sure you get sufficient sleep the night before and don't pile too many interviews into one day if you can avoid it. Second, sufficient preparation tends to allow you to feel more relaxed and positive when you are being interviewed, which will make you come across as more likable. Finally, remember this is a "sales presentation"! Research consistently indicates that nonverbal communication is even more important than verbal communication in presentation contexts. So practice, practice, practice!

Verbal Communication Tips

Verbal communication that enables you to stand out among the crowd of applicants includes both the words that constitute your responses and questions, as well as how you deliver those responses and questions. The following are a few tips that are noted on the interview evaluation form in Chapter 10:

- *Project a pleasant tone of voice.* Speak loudly enough to be heard but not too overpowering; avoid a monotone delivery (think of Ben Stein as the teacher in the movie *Ferris Bueller's Day Off*: "Bueller? Bueller? Fry? Fry?").

- *Avoid filler words.* You need to learn how to speak professionally; avoid repetitive use of "uh," "um," "you know," and "like." Don't be afraid of momentary pauses or silence to collect your thoughts before you respond to a question.

- *Avoid credibility robbers.* Don't undermine yourself by using the words "maybe," "I guess," "perhaps," or "little"; while you should not embellish your accomplishments, neither should you diminish them.

- *Use positive words and phrases.* Don't drain the energy of the interview by focusing on the negative; stay positive and use words that convey passion and excitement.

- *Use correct grammar.* If you are a college graduate (or soon to be one) then there will be an expectation that you can articulate your thoughts in a grammatically sound manner. Make sure this is true even when you are nervous.

- *Remain focused.* The interview is not a monologue; make sure you heard the question correctly and if you don't understand the questions, ask the interviewer for clarification. Then give a concise response that answers the question in 3 minutes or less. Do *not* ramble, especially with the "Tell me about yourself" question.

- *Demonstrate a sense of humor.* I think that a little injection of humor, even self-effacing humor, leaves a positive impression on the interviewer. It can suggest that you would be fun to work with, have a positive attitude, and that you do not take yourself too seriously. As with most behaviors, however, overdoing it becomes distracting, so use moderation.

Now let's transition to the responses themselves. In general, you want to come across as prepared and interested in the company, knowledgeable about the profession, and confident about your potential fit and ability to add value to the company. Providing specific answers and concrete examples is always better than sticking to generic responses. Driving down to particular responses, you cannot anticipate every question you will be asked in an interview but there are many frequently asked questions that you should have at least thought through. Here are 10 common questions[4] and some ideas for how to respond to them.

Question 1   Tell me about yourself.
This is quite likely the most frequently asked first question in interviews. Part of the purpose in this general question is to assess your communication tendencies (e.g., how talkative are you?). Another purpose is for the interviewer to get an initial feel for what is important to you because the assumption is that you will emphasize important points about yourself. Don't ramble with this question, and don't start at the beginning (I was born in . . .). Limit the response to 3 minutes or less, and direct it toward those qualities that you want the interviewer to remember about you.

Question 2   Why are you interested in working here?
The interviewer wants to understand your aspirations and to assess the potential fit for you in the company. This question also allows applicants to demonstrate the homework they have done to research the company. Also, make sure that your response is not self-serving in nature (e.g., "I love the higher-than-market salaries and corporate perks that you offer your employees"), even if those benefits are enticing to you. Focus on the fit issue. If you can connect your short-term career goals with the needs of the employer, then you will separate yourself from other applicants.

Question 3   Why have you chosen this particular field?
This is somewhat similar to the previous question. The interviewer is trying to understand what makes you tick, how knowledgeable you are in your field, and how your skills and passions will fit with the company's culture and direction.

---

[4] Adapted from *Job choices* (2004), by the National Association of Colleges and Employers, p. 43.

Question 4   Describe your best or worst boss.

Interviewers may ask this for a couple of reasons. The first and most common reason is just to hear what you think about past pleasant and unpleasant work relationships. Never use the interview to vent or rail on past bosses (no matter how incompetent you think they may have been). You never know who is in the interviewer's professional network and discussing all the negatives about a past boss comes across as whiny and unprofessional. This is a question where a more general answer may actually be better. This answer may be something like "My boss and I were not on the same page with the direction (or scope) of my position and responsibilities." A second reason for asking this question may be to try to match you better with one of multiple managers in the company. In larger companies, there could be openings in multiple offices, so the fit between your preferred supervisor's working style would be important information. Answer honestly about the characteristics of your best boss. Never demean a former boss. If pushed, you can be relatively specific but tactful about the deficiencies of the "worst boss."

Question 5   What is your major strength/weakness?

This is a very common question. Let's take the strength question first. The interviewer wants to know how well you know yourself. If it takes you a while to come up with your major strength, that is a problem. My suggestion is to think before the interview about three to five strengths that you would bring to this company. Then look at the position requirements and cite the strength that is most desired for this particular position. The weakness question is a different animal. Never respond that you cannot think of any right off the top of your head. This is an arrogant, ignorant response because each of us has multiple weaknesses. You can use some quality that could be perceived by some individuals as a strength (e.g., "I tend to be a perfectionist about high-quality work and that can sometimes come across as overbearing to coworkers"). My first suggestion for answering this question is to make sure that you know what three to five of your most prominent weaknesses are. Second, know the position requirements and do *not* cite as a weakness an area that is demanded heavily in the job. Third, after you mention the weakness, indicate what you are doing or have done to improve that attribute. Employers know that you will not be perfect, but they want to know that you are coachable and willing to improve on problematic areas.

Question 6   Give me an example of a problem you encountered either in school or at work, and explain how you solved it.

This is an example of a behavioral-based interview question. Use the SAR process presented in Chapter 4 to relate (briefly) a specific problem situation, the actions *you* took to solve the problem, and the outcomes of the solution. Other common behavioral-based questions relate to leadership, team development, and customer service situations. Practice the SAR process.

Question 7   Where do you see yourself in 3 years?

A very tough question for many applicants. How do you tell the prospective employer that you plan to start a family within the next three years? You don't. How do you indicate that you plan to pursue a graduate degree after two years? You don't. Of course, the interviewer wants to understand how you view your future with this organization. The hiring and initial training costs for new employees are substantial, and companies want to ensure that they get some return on that investment. Add the words "with this organization" silently to the original question. If you have a strong knowledge of the company's internal structure and professional career paths you can answer with greater specificity. Otherwise, you can throw the question back to the interviewer in this manner: "If I meet or exceed the performance expectations for this position, where can I be with your company in 3 years?" This is an appropriate question because it will lead into a discussion of opportunities for advancement and the company's performance evaluation process, both of which are facets of the company you will want to clearly understand.

Question 8   *If you were an animal, which animal would you be, and why?*
What a strange question, you say? Well, this question or one of its variations ("If you were a car . . ." "If you were a city . . ." "If you were a song . . .") is being more frequently asked. What purposes does this type of question serve? It accomplishes at least two objectives. First, it shows the interviewer how you handle stress (or at least the unexpected) and how you think on your feet. So don't get flustered with this type of question. Second, it can tell the interviewer something else about who you are, your personality, and how you view yourself. I wouldn't spend a lot of time on preparing for these types of questions but you need to provide an answer and then give a meaningful reason for your response. Ideally, the reason will reinforce a personal attribute that would contribute to successful performance of the position.

Question 9   *What was the last book you read?*
Focus on both professional and personal books. The interviewer wants to assess how you keep current in your professional field. If you have read something outside of your line of work recently that will show the interviewer the breadth of your appetite for learning, it is not inappropriate to bring it up. Be careful with citing any books that disclose personal information that you don't want the employer to know at that stage of the hiring process. The bottom line is to make sure you are reading books and/or periodicals that keep you informed about industry and occupational trends and issues.

Question 10   *What questions do you have for me?*
The interviewer asks this question to signal that any structured interview questions are now completed and the interview is likely coming to a close in the next 5 to 10 minutes. You should always have at least three insightful questions that evidence your research before you come to the interview. It is doubtful that the interviewer will have answered all three in the course of your conversation. You should *never* pass on asking any questions. Show your intellectual curiosity to learn.

 TREK TASK 26

RESPONSES TO COMMON INTERVIEW QUESTIONS

Review these 10 common questions. Prepare some written notes about how you would answer questions 1 and 5 (you will almost always be asked those in a real interview). Don't rehearse a verbatim response, but write down key points that you would want to emphasize.

BE-ATTITUDES

Regardless of your beliefs about Jesus Christ, he is widely accepted as a phenomenal teacher. In his most well-known sermon, the Sermon on the Mount, Jesus presented several principles that have been referred to as the Beatitudes (e.g., "Blessed are the meek: for they shall inherit the earth.").[5] Biblical scholars have suggested that this list of principles constitute the recipe for a successful life, a life of peace and happiness. Well, I have come up with 10 "BE" statements (hence the term *BE-attitudes*) that will provide you with greater success in interviewing.

1. *BE yourself.* There is no long-term benefit in trying to be something you are not during the interview. If you try to be who you think the company wants and it is not really you, then good interviewers will detect the inconsistency or it will come across as a forced attempt. Second, if you get the job based on false impressions, then the expectations the employer has of you will be difficult to meet. You can fool someone for 30 to 60 minutes in an interview but not for weeks and months of daily employment. Know yourself well, and be the best possible "you" during those interviews.

2. *BE prepared.* My old Boy Scout training comes through again here; you will make an indelible impression on your interviewer if you have come prepared. Review Chapter 10, bring the right physical materials, and remember the necessary information to shine.

3. *BE focused.* One of the biggest problems that novice interviewees experience is a lack of focus in their responses. Part of that difficulty is that in their initial excitement about landing an interview they forget exactly what they hope to accomplish. You want to stand out positively in the interviewer's mind. This is done more effectively if your responses emphasize some common themes that you want the interviewer to remember about you (and your brand). Also, stay focused on this interview—don't get ahead of yourself by thinking about future interviews or other job offers.

4. *BE inquisitive.* Interviewers want to find people who can identify and solve tough problems. One of the characteristics they look for is intellectual curiosity. You can demonstrate this in the interview by asking good questions, especially follow-up questions that show you have been listening to the interviewer. Make it a point to leave the interviewer with a genuine impression that you enjoy learning new things.

5. *BE enthusiastic.* We discussed this attitude in Chapter 2. Employers want to hire people who will energize others with their enthusiasm, not drain others with their pessimism or apathy. Smile, demonstrate passion, talk positively about the company's future and your future with the company. Of course, this attitude is hard to fake if this is a company and/or position for which you are not honestly excited. Maybe you are there primarily to gain some experience interviewing. Make sure that you withhold judgment about the company and position until you have learned sufficient information. In the meantime, be enthusiastic.

---

[5] Matthew 5:3–12, in the New Testament of the Holy Bible (King James Version).

6. *BE confident.* It is fairly easy for interviewers to spot those applicants who are uncertain about their capabilities. Your previous research and preparation for the interview should help you feel confident about the outcomes of the interview. Don't mistake confidence and cockiness. Most employers don't appreciate arrogance (e.g., "Weaknesses . . . I don't really have any that come to mind"), but they do want to see that you believe in yourself and are reasonably assertive in meeting objectives, including your own career objectives.

7. *BE concise.* While good interviewers expect to spend significant portions of the interview listening to your responses, they do not appreciate rambling remarks. In fact, if any of your answers starts to exceed 3 minutes then you need to wrap it up and move on. Use simple, precise, and concise terms to showcase what you have to offer to the employer.

8. *BE professional.* There is no substitute for this attitude in the interview. It is an overall assessment that the interviewer makes about how you would interact with coworkers, managers, and customers if the company were to hire you. It consists of how you carry yourself (poise and composure under stress), your communication habits, respectful behaviors toward others, and your appearance.

9. *BE honest. Never* fabricate accomplishments or lie about your experiences or qualifications. For example, don't say that financial analysis is one of your strengths when it is not. This point also relates to my advice about integrity with your résumé. Interviewers will sometimes attempt to verify information on your résumé during the interview by asking you more specific questions. If your answers make it clear that you embellished or outright lied on your résumé, kiss the job good-bye. This does not mean, however, that you must disclose all facts surrounding a question asked by the interviewer. For example, if you are asked why you left your previous job and the real reason is that the company had terrible management, you can't say it exactly like that.

10. *BE on time.* Remember that there is no excuse for being late to an interview. Arrive 5 to 10 minutes early at the designated interview location and be ready for the interview. If it is a telephone interview then make sure you are ready to receive the call 5 minutes before the scheduled time. This is a first impression that interviewers definitely remember.

▲🚶🚶 TREK TASK 27
IMPROVING YOUR BE-ATTITUDES

Review these 10 BE-attitudes. Think about recent interviews and identify two BE-attitudes that you need to improve. Write down a specific improvement plan for each one and review it with a trusted network member.

CLOSING THE INTERVIEW

What separates outstanding salespersons from good ones? Both groups are well informed and well prepared to discuss their products. They demonstrate enthusiasm and effectively answer questions. They are courteous and professional. But the outstanding salesperson knows how to close the deal. You need to know how to effectively close the interview. I have to admit that I didn't learn this principle very well until the past few years.

After the interviewer has asked you for your questions and then responded to them, many applicants at that point will thank the interviewer for the opportunity to meet. The interviewer will thank the applicant for coming and for the person's time. And then those famous words, "We'll let you know." More savvy interviewers will remember to spell out the timing of the next steps in the hiring process, but not all interviewers do that. You may have time constraints based on the interviewer's schedule, but you need to take the brief moments to "close the deal." How do you do this? Here are the basic elements needed to close the interview:

- Remind the interviewer of what value you could bring to the company. One of my former students, Dace Murphy, provided an excellent example of what I am talking about. He said that he likes to say the following:

   I believe that there is an excellent fit here. Your company has a lot of the characteristics I'm looking for, and I'm confident that I could add considerable value to your organization. I will look forward to hearing from you! Thank you again for meeting me this afternoon.

- Ask a question to assess the interviewer's impressions of you now that the interview has reached its conclusion. The following sage advice was provided by my good friend and careers enthusiast, Bob Uda:

   Never leave the interview without looking your interviewer straight in the eyes and asking this all-important question: *"Now that you've read my resume and interviewed me, from everything that I have said, do you feel that my background and capabilities meet your requirements?"* Invariably, most people that interview you will say, "Yes." If they hesitate for a fraction of a second, that will give you a clue that you are not the top person for the job. Never leave an interview without receiving a definite impression as to whether or not you will be selected for the job.[6]

- If the interviewer has not yet told you the next steps in the process, ask about them.

- Thank the interviewer again for her time, consideration of your qualifications, and candid responses to your questions. Then indicate that you may have a couple of follow-up questions that you would like to ask her. Ask for the interviewer's preferred method of communication (e-mail or phone) and note that somewhere in your portfolio or on the interviewer's business card. Don't leave the interview until you have completed this step. A graceful exit (don't trip or get lost) from the interview location is icing on the cake.

---

[6] Uda, R.T. (2003). *What hue is your bungee cord?* Universe.com, p. 25.

Improving your interviewing is key to successfully getting your foot in the door with an organization. Using our mountaineering analogy, it provides you with a foothold from which to launch your assault on the mountain's summit. It puts you on safe and stable ground until you are prepared to renew your climb.

Before we leave interviewing and this crucial segment of the career trek, there is one more chapter that you need to digest. Chapter 12 discusses what you do after the interview (interview follow-up activities are neglected by many applicants), particularly related to interview follow-up activities and job offers (negotiating and evaluating them).

▲🚶🚶 TREK LIST

☐ **FIRST IMPRESSIONS**   I know how important they are in the interview and I am aware of how I come across in the first 3 to 5 minutes of interviews.

☐ **QUESTIONS**   I have reviewed common interview questions and considered my best responses to those questions. I have also developed three to five good questions that I want to ask the interviewer.

☐ **BE-ATTITUDES**   I know which of the 10 that I need to work on the most so I can really shine in the interview.

☐ **THE CLOSER**   I have learned the four key steps of closing an interview effectively. I will practice those steps in mock and real interviews.

Following Up
the Interview
Negotiating and
Evaluating Job Offers

In a tight job market, multiple offers sound too good to be true. So what's the problem? Choose the one that pays the most and move on, right? Wrong. If you don't take the time to evaluate the offers, you could find yourself searching for a job again in no time.

—*Carole Martin (Monster contributing writer)*

You have just completed your interview and hopefully did not hear the interviewer say, in his best Donald Trump voice, "You're fired!" Your work is now done, right? The ball is in the company's court? *No!* While it is certainly true that the company has the decision-making authority at this stage of the process to evaluate your candidacy for the position, the steps *you* take following the interview can further differentiate you from other applicants. Your effective follow-up activities will continue to stamp an impression of utmost professionalism on the minds of those who have interviewed you—a critical impression as they compare otherwise qualified applicants. Some of these activities should seem obvious but many applicants are oblivious to them and neglect to send even a thank-you e-mail.

The objectives of this chapter are the following:

- To provide you with a checklist of important interview follow-up activities
- To present guidelines for effectively negotiating job offers
- To suggest a process for evaluating job offers, especially when you have multiple offers.
- To explain briefly the importance of leaving your current position on good footing.

THE NEGLECTED ART OF FOLLOW-UP

The common feelings after an interview include relief (phew, I'm out of the spotlight!), exhilaration (if you thought the interview went really well), or frustration (if you thought the interview bombed). Unfortunately, at this point many applicants will just wash their hands of the interview process and passively await the outcomes of the interview. That is the wrong approach. Those who interviewed you are human beings, after all. Their memories fade and they do not retain perfect information about each applicant. So the following is a checklist of activities you should complete to effectively follow up after your interview.

Interview Follow-up Checklist

- ☐ *Conduct an interview audit.* Evaluate your interview from preparation to closing.
- ☐ *Send a thank-you note or letter.* Do this within 24 hours after the interview.
- ☐ *Map out the next steps.* Review what the interviewer said as you closed your interview.
- ☐ *Seek feedback for improvement.* Complete this step especially if you are not receiving any call-backs from your interviews.
- ☐ *Update your network.* Let your references know where you are in the process.

The first step is to evaluate how you did in the interview. You can formally do this using the evaluation form at the end of Chapter 10, or you can informally reflect upon the interview. Start before the interview. How prepared was I? How did I feel when I arrived at the interview location? What responses could have been improved? What questions surprised me, or caused me to struggle for a response? How was my body language throughout the interview? How effective were my questions? How did I close the interview? What do I think now about the potential fit of this job and company with what I am looking for? What do I believe my chances are to continue to the next phase of the hiring process? Make sure that you conduct this audit of your interviewing skills while the interview is still fresh in your mind.

Within 24 hours after the interview (or interviews), you *must* send a note or letter of appreciation to your interviewer. *Sending an effective thank-you letter is the most vital of all of these follow-up activities.* "Writing powerful thank-you letters is not just a formality. Thank-you letters are marketing tools that can have tremendous value in moving your candidacy forward and positioning you above the competition."[1] If you had multiple interviewers, send each one a thank-you note. You might think this is overkill because you already thanked the interviewer when you closed the interview. You might think that—but you would be wrong! Many applicants overlook this step. Students ask me, "Is it okay to send a thank-you e-mail instead?" I tell them that an e-mail is better than nothing, but an actual letter or card is always better. An e-mail note may be beneficial when you want to follow up sooner with some important information, such an accomplishment you omitted or a response to an interviewer's concern. Send the e-mail, but send a hard-copy thank-you letter as well.

After you have sent your thank-you letters, step back and breathe for a moment. Now think about your next steps. How badly do you want this job now that you have learned more about it? What was the interviewer's reaction to your interview? What are the next steps in the process? When should I contact the

---

[1] Enelow, W. S. http://interview.monster.com/articles/thankyou/ (accessed April 2004).

interviewer if I have not yet received any communication about my candidacy? These are questions you need to consider to map out your strategy to continue to show the company that you are the best person for the job.

If you think that the interview went poorly or you have been rejected for the position, consider asking the interviewer (by phone) for some candid feedback. This can be done in a tactful, nonobnoxious way. Don't grovel or argue that the company made a mistake. You can say something like this, "I appreciated the opportunity to interview for this position, and I respect that your decision was to hire another applicant. So that I can improve myself professionally, can you offer me any feedback on my interviewing skills so that I can present myself better in the future?" Most interviewers will provide some feedback that will be valuable for you. Plus, you might leave the positive impression that you are always trying to improve. This may lead to an unsolicited invitation by that company for another position opening at a later time. Monster.com offers some helpful additional guidelines when asking for interview feedback.[2]

Finally, last but not least, keep your closest network members (at least your references) updated on how your search process is proceeding. This is also a good opportunity to benefit from their wisdom. For example, suppose you didn't feel that you handled the "What would your boss say is your greatest weakness?" question very well. Ask someone in your network whose interviewing skills you respect for advice. Remember that these individuals care about you and your career. Seek their advice and share your successes and challenges with them.

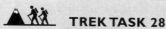 **TREK TASK 28**

INTERVIEW FOLLOW-UP CHECKLIST

Complete the follow-up checklist. At the very least, make sure you have sent your thank-you letters. Prepare for the next interview, whether it is with the same company or not.

NEGOTIATING THE JOB OFFER

Your intensive preparation, interviewing skills, and attention to vital follow-up activities have paid off. The prospective employer makes you an initial offer to accept the position. Now comes the critical step of offer negotiations. You need to better understand what, when, and how to negotiate.

Negotiable Elements of the Offer

Many job seekers mistakenly focus on negotiating only the salary element of job offers. Several other elements of a job offer can be minimally or extensively negotiated. Some benefits, such as vacation time and healthcare benefits (medical and dental coverage) are set by company policies and are less negotiable. However,

---

[2] Martin, C. http://interview.monster.com/articles/feedback/ (accessed April 2004).

even vacation time can be negotiated within reasonable parameters for legitimate reasons. When I was considering joining Andersen Consulting, the company policy was that employees would start to accrue a certain number of hours each 2-week pay period until they attained the 80 hours of paid vacation that was standard for all new employees. However, my wedding was coming up soon after my start date and I wanted to take two weeks off for my out-of-state wedding and subsequent honeymoon. I negotiated for and received an advance on my vacation time so that those vacation days were paid instead of unpaid.

Other negotiable (but sometimes neglected) elements of the offer include

- Signing bonuses (more common when there are labor market shortages and for higher-level positions)
- Stock options (for many companies, either pre- or post-IPO)
- Relocation expenses (some companies pay all, others will pay up to a certain amount)
- Placement assistance for your spouse/partner
- Flexible scheduling/telecommuting options (popular in metropolitan areas)
- Severance packages (usually for higher-level positions)
- Performance and salary review time frames (if companies start new hires at lower-than-market salaries they will often promise a 60-day or 90-day review for possible salary increase)
- Other perks (professional memberships, fitness club dues, company car, cellular phones, laptops, and other technology tools or applications)

Crucial to your effective offer negotiations is knowing exactly what you want and understanding what the company can realistically do for you. For example, when I negotiated my offer to come to Cal State San Marcos, I expected (accurately, I might add) that there would be minimal negotiability of the base salary. Public, not-for-profit, unionized organizations tend to have very rigid pay scales. However, I could (and did) negotiate for a larger reimbursement of my relocation expenses and a somewhat easier first-semester teaching load (so that I could finish the editing of my dissertation and acclimate myself and my family to the new area). The bottom line is to keep in mind that you need to consider all aspects of what the prospective employer can offer, not just money.

Timing of Offer Negotiations

When does the negotiation process begin? *Negotiations, especially related to compensation, do not begin until after an offer has been made.* My point is that you should not start debating the various elements of a potential offer until an actual offer has been provided to you by the employer. In fact, career experts commonly hold that you always want the employer to bring up salary figures first (make sure, though, that you know what salary range is acceptable given your needs and market research). Once a formal offer has been extended you may go through some iteration of offers and counteroffers. This tends to happen more with upper-level positions than with lower-level positions. Eventually, a final offer will be extended to you by the employer. You will then have to make a decision of whether to accept or reject the final offer. The timing of that decision varies depending on how many other viable candidates the employer perceives and the urgency of filling the position. The company may give you as much as 2 to 3 weeks or as little as 2 to 3 days to decide.

How to Negotiate Effectively

Even if you know when and what elements to negotiate, you still need to learn how to do so effectively. Lee Miller, former senior vice president of human resources for Barneys New York and author of *Get More Money on Your Next Job: 25 Proven Strategies for Getting More Money, Better Benefits and Greater Job Security,* wrote an article that identified 11 basic commandments for better job offer negotiations.[3] While these were presented at the height of the strong economy in the late 1990s, their validity is still high from my experience. Here are Miller's negotiation commandments with a few of his own comments from the article.

COMMANDMENT	LEE MILLER'S COMMENTS
Be prepared.	The more information you have about your market value and the prospective employer, the greater your likelihood of success. This is the first commandment because it's the most important. . . . Time spent learning how to negotiate and preparing for negotiations may be the best investment you'll ever make.
Recognize that employment negotiations are different.	[Y]our future success may depend on that person [with whom you are negotiating]. So, while you want to negotiate the best possible deal, you need to so in a way that doesn't damage your image. At the same time, the employer's primary concern isn't negotiating the least expensive compensation package it can get away with. Rather, their focus will be on getting you to accept the job.
Understand your needs and those of the employer.	To be successful in this type of negotiation, you need to examine your priorities. What do you really want? . . . By recognizing what an employer can and can't do, you'll be able to determine what issues you should press.
Understand the dynamics of the particular negotiations.	Sometimes you'll have skills that are in great demand. And sometimes, you may be one of several qualified candidates the company would be happy to hire. Sizing up the situation and

---

[3] Miller, L. Eleven commandments for smart negotiating (available from www.careerjournal.com).

understanding the relative position of each party will help you determine when to press your advantage and when to back off.

Never lie, but use the truth to your advantage.

It's not only wrong to lie, but in employment negotiations, it's ineffective . . . sooner or later you're likely to be caught . . . even if you don't lose the offer . . . your credibility will always be suspect. On the other hand, total candor won't be rewarded. You're under no obligation to blurt out everything you know.

Understand the role fairness plays in the process.

The guiding principle for most employers when negotiating is fairness. . . . Appeals to fairness are your most powerful weapon. . . . Your prospective employer will want you to accept its offer and feel that you've been treated fairly.

Use uncertainty to your advantage.

The more information you convey to a potential employer about your bottom line, the more likely it will limit what you get. . . . While they may not offer you as little as they can get away with, if you've divulged too much information, they likely won't offer you as much as they might have otherwise. By not disclosing exactly what your current compensation is or exactly what it would take to get you to leave your job, you'll force a potential employer to make its best offer.

Be creative.

Look for different ways to achieve your objectives. . . . You'll also be able to find creative "trades" that allow you to withdraw requests that might be problematic to the company in return for improvements in areas where the company has more flexibility.

Focus on your goals, not on winning.

Too often in negotiations, the act of winning becomes more important than achieving your goals. And it's also important not to make your future boss feel as if he's lost in the negotiations. You'll have gained little by negotiating a good deal if you alienate your future boss in the process.

Know when to quit bargaining.

The one sure way to lose everything you've obtained is to be greedy. . . . Being perceived as greedy or unreasonable may cause the deal to fall apart. Even if it doesn't, you'll have done immeasurable harm to your career.

Never forget that employment is an ongoing relationship.

Job negotiations are the starting point for your career with a company. Get too little and you're disadvantaged throughout your career there; push too hard and you can sour the relationship before it begins.

Eleven is quite a few commandments to remember (God gave Moses only 10!), but an underlying point to his guidelines is that the employment negotiation process should not be a win–lose endeavor. While applicants may think otherwise, most companies are not trying to lowball the individuals who they most want to join their ranks. Neither you nor the company wants to start the relationship off on the wrong foot. Just keep thinking how you can help the company and still obtain your fair and reasonable objectives. Let me end this section with just *four negotiating principles* that you should take with you:

1. Know what you are worth. Do your homework so that you know the fairness of the initial offer.
2. Know what you want and what elements are negotiable for you.
3. You are actually worth the offer you accept (this is my friend Bob Uda's favorite negotiating statement, hereafter called Uda's maxim).
4. Never burn bridges in the negotiating process, but especially those bridges you have not yet completely crossed.

 TREK TASK 29
TIPS FOR NEGOTIATING JOB OFFERS

Go to www.google.com or www.metacrawler.com and enter in *negotiating job offers* as your search term. Go to three to five different Web sites and read a few of the brief articles you find on negotiations tips. Write down in the Notes portion of your portfolio any key insights. Remember Uda's maxim: You are worth what you accept.

EVALUATING JOB OFFERS

Having discussed negotiating principles for a single job offer, what should you do if you are in the fortunate position of having to choose from multiple offers? Because each and every job offer is at least somewhat different, it is very difficult to give you any prescriptive advice about how to select the best offer. But I'll be daring and unafraid and suggest a process to help you evaluate them; all you need is a blank sheet of paper.

First, you have to *write down the five most important criteria* you want satisfied by any selected position. There are many factors to choose from and they tend to fall into six major categories:

- *Job/position.* Duties, level of autonomy, stress, key objectives, performance expectations, amount of expected travel and overtime, working conditions
- *Organization.* Culture, future outlook, opportunities for advancement, professional development/training, reputation
- *Geography.* Location, potential relocations, relocation expenses, quality of life, commute time, cost of living
- *Salary and benefits.* Base salary, frequency and amount of typical raises, bonuses, stock options, medical and dental insurance, profit sharing, 401(k), retirement, paid vacation, paid holidays, company-specific perks
- *Relationships.* Impact on significant nonwork relationships, reporting relationships, coworkers, key customers
- *Personal.* Hobbies, life goals, values alignment, gut instinct

Second, *write the names of the employers* who have offered you positions as columns at the top of the page.

Third, *rate each offer according to your five criteria.* This process is flexible as you can choose from several different rating schemes. You can rate each offer from 1 to10, or rate them as "acceptable" or "not acceptable" for each criterion. Alternatively, you can use a High, Moderate, or Low classification for how well each offer satisfies each criterion.

Fourth, *review your grid and make a decision.* Look at the relative merits of each offer and consider the overall implications of accepting any of the offers. You may find that the only truly important criterion is your first one. For example, the geographic location may be the critical factor, or it may be the organization's culture that is most essential to your decision.

Two final thoughts are in order here: (a) don't underestimate the importance of gut instinct when it comes to making significant career decisions (or life decisions for that matter); and (b) be *very* careful about choosing an offer based solely on a better salary. My value system offers me substantial evidence that there is a grander purpose in life than the small slice with which we are typically aware. If you experience confusion or concern in your gut about a particular career choice, it is very likely the wrong path. Conversely, if you feel peace and passion about a choice, it is very likely a path you want to pursue. To my second point, I have never allowed the money to be *the* deciding factor in any of my career-related decisions. Too many individuals, especially those right out of college, overemphasize the money and ignore issues of cultural fit, nature of the job itself, advancement opportunities, and impact on important relationships. I'm not saying the "green" isn't important; it just isn't the most important in my book.

Once you have made a decision about which offer to accept, you have a couple of unfinished responsibilities. First, you should verbally inform the employer whose offer you are accepting about your decision. Clarify the key points of the offer and request that the offer be stated in writing (if the formal offer was not already provided to you in written form). Second, you should contact the other employers and inform them that you have decided not to accept their offers. Express gratitude and wish them future success. Continue to be professional and don't rub any employer's nose in the rejection. Rejected employers may ask you to indicate the company with which you have accepted an offer. You can choose to do so, but don't disclose the terms of the offer.

LEAVING ON GOOD FOOTING

The final concept of this chapter is that you should act with professionalism in leaving your current employer, if you have one. Regardless of your attitudes toward your current employer, you should leave the right way. What is the right way? Give your employer at least two weeks' notice before your anticipated last day on the job. If your activities are critical to the company and your position will be difficult to replace, then *give your employer ample notice so that decision makers can prepare for your departure.* Express gratitude to your coworkers. Make sure that customers are transitioned effectively. Leave your position better than you found it when you started. Don't talk negatively about your current company or brag to your coworkers about the greener pastures that you have found. Finish strong and keep your mind focused on your current responsibilities. Your future responsibilities will arrive quickly enough.

TREK LIST

☐ **INTERVIEW FOLLOW-UP**   Review the checklist and use it!

☐ **OFFER NEGOTIATIONS**   I know what aspects of my offer are negotiable, and I have learned some key points for being a better negotiator. I have talked with an experienced network member about offer negotiations.

☐ **OFFER EVALUATION**   I have specified my main criteria for evaluating the job and given thorough examination to all elements of the offer, not just base pay.

☐ **BURNING BRIDGES**   I will never do it!

PART IV

REACHING THE SUMMIT

Secretly, I dreamed of ascending Everest myself one day; for more than a decade it remained a burning ambition. By the time I was in my early twenties climbing had become the focus of my existence to the exclusion of almost everything else. Achieving the summit of a mountain was tangible, immutable, concrete. The incumbent hazards lent the activity a seriousness of purpose that was sorely missing from the rest of my life.

—*Jon Krakauer (Into Thin Air, p. 23)*

Have you ever watched someone work (or play) who is at the summit of their profession? Have you seen Tiger Woods in the final round at one of the major golf tournaments? Do you remember actors or musicians performing at the peaks of their careers? It is a beautiful thing to watch. Pursuit of your career summit will likely require your best concentration and focus, your persistence in the face of adversity, and the consistent alignment of your best skills and passions with an environment that provides you the regular opportunity to use those skills. All that we have learned together on the career trek is meant to prepare you to go for the summit not to be stranded on the side of the mountain.

This last part of the career trek emphasizes what happens after you land the job you want. Obtaining it can be difficult, but keeping it in today's competitive work environment is tougher still. To help you progress in your career to the summit of what you are striving to become, the following chapters will address

- Tips for success in your first year of new employment, plus suggestions for longer-term career success (Chapter 13)
- Facing and making tough career decisions along your path to the summit (Chapter 14)

- The advantages and disadvantages of mentoring, plus other developmental options that you should utilize to continually develop your skills (Chapter 15)

Trust someone who is still striving to reach the summit—the journey is fraught with twists and turns, but if you are doing what you love, it is an exhilarating climb up the mountain.

Rules for Career Success

DILBERT: © Scott Adams/Dist. by United Feature Syndicate, Inc.

I hope the preceding chapters have assisted you in landing an excellent job, with an offer that is fair, and you are now enthusiastically preparing for your first day on the job. Be prepared, for the saying often mentioned with new marriages is applicable with new employers: "The honeymoon's over!" Even with great companies, once you have accepted an offer and show up for your first day of work, the relationship has changed. Now you are expected to perform.

You have obtained a good job, but that is *not* the summit of your career (hopefully!). There is still more mountain to climb, and the next three chapters will attempt to help you do so. In this chapter you will learn the following concepts:

- Starting strong "out of the gate" (making your first year count)
- Rules for career success (Moses' 12 Commandments)
- Setting SMART goals to move your career forward
- Measuring your progress using two tests: the McKRT and the PBET

MAKING YOUR FIRST YEAR A SUCCESS

Positive first impressions are important in the interviewing process and they are equally important when you join a new organization. You definitely want to perform in ways that make your boss and coworkers glad you were hired. In some organizations (typically larger corporations) you will not be expected to make instant contributions while others will expect instant impact. I grew up in Salt Lake City, Utah, and because of my proximity to the Rocky Mountains, you would expect me to know something about skiing. Sheepishly, I admit that I have gone skiing only once in my life. It was a harrowing experience made worse because the company I rented my equipment from gave me two left-footed ski boots. I fell over and over again (do you hear tears and soft violins playing in the background?). But what I have observed about competitive skiing is that downhill races are often won or lost by how the skier comes "out of the gate." As a new employee, you need to start fast and in the right direction out of the gate. Here are some points to consider for a fast start:

- Clarify your boss's expectations and obtain a clear understanding of her top two or three priorities.
- Demonstrate the utmost integrity, professionalism, and positive attitude.
- Perform exceptionally well those activities for which you have ownership. You should attempt to exceed the expectations of others.
- Seek feedback from others concerning your job performance. Ensure that formal performance review schedules are fulfilled, but do this in a tactful way.
- Start internal networking by building bridges with your "internal customers."
- Get one or multiple mentors inside your new organization. This will be covered in greater detail in Chapter 15.
- Show up on time, be someone others can count on, and work really hard.

When I joined Andersen Consulting the advice I received was "to show that you are competent in your job." My coworkers indicated that nothing else really mattered if your performance was subpar for your most critical responsibilities. So I echo that counsel to you. Reread the point made in the preceding list about performing exceptionally well. Renowned business leader, Jack Welch, former CEO of General Electric, expressed that he almost left GE early in his career but was persuaded to stay at the company by his boss's boss. That executive held a

 TREK TASK 30

CLARIFY YOUR BOSS'S EXPECTATIONS

Clarify expectations. Make sure you understand what your boss wants in terms of your role and performance. Perform your most critical tasks to exceed expectations.

positive impression of Jack because in all of Jack's tasks in his first two years with GE, Jack had worked extra hard to exceed expectations. You can start doing this now in your collegiate courses—clarify your professors' expectations for specific assignments and exceed them. You will develop a reputation right now that will serve you well in the future.

RULES FOR LONG-TERM CAREER SUCCESS

It is challenging and, I dare say, ambitious to try to prescribe to you any specific rules for career success. In part, that is because each person can have substantially different definitions of career success. Also, each career is built upon innumerable small actions and decisions along the way. Many successful individuals talk about how lucky and fortunate they were to have been in the right place at the right time. Nevertheless, I present you with a thorough set of rules for your consideration.

Moses' 12 Career Commandments

The following 12 rules have been identified by Dr. Barbara Moses, author of the book *Career Intelligence: The 12 New Rules for Work and Life Success.*[1] For each of her "commandments" I have provided some commentary to help you understand how this pertains to your eventual career success.

MOSES' COMMANDMENT	AUTHOR'S COMMENTS
Ensure your marketability	Very few companies offer explicit or implicit job security, so you always need to assess your marketability in case you become the next layoff victim. Networking can help you, as can effective training and professional development. Moses says, "Examine the work you are currently doing and ask yourself if it is providing experiences or new skills that enhance your marketability. If not, seek out assignments and projects that offer you opportunities that will make you more marketable in the future."[2]
Think globally	We live in a global economy; in fact, I've heard it suggested that countries are like suburbs of a global metropolis. The implication is that you have an advantage if you know other languages and cultures and have spent significant time in another country. This is becoming an increasingly important career success factor.

---

[1] Moses, B. (1998). *Career intelligence: The 12 new rules for work and life success.* San Francisco: Berrett-Koehler Publishers. See Chapter 9 (pp. 169–200).

[2] Ibid., p. 171.

Communicate powerfully and persuasively	Technology has expanded the communication channels available to us but has also led to information overload and a greater sense of insufficient time. So our communications with others must be effective and persuasive. Moses adds, "One of the critical skills for career success will be being able to communicate graphically, compellingly, and quickly in both oral and in written form."[3]
Never stop learning	Completing your formal degree does not mean that learning ends. You *must* continue to develop new knowledge and skills to ensure your marketability. Ask your employer about any tuition reimbursement opportunities and consider professional courses and certifications that you can take on your own time.
Understand business trends	You need to know yourself to enjoy career success, but you also need to know your business. Knowledge is power! What do you know about potential trends in your profession and/or industry? What business periodicals do you read, either online or in print form? Remember that as you are climbing the mountain the terrain is dynamic, not static—you need to stay current on changes to the landscape.
Prepare for competencies and roles, not jobs	Job titles come and go. Think more about the roles you play in your jobs and the transferable competencies you have honed instead of the title you hold. Moses states, "Define yourself by what you do and how you get it done, not by your job title."[4]
Look to the future	While you should not choose a particular career path solely on its projected future demand, you should at least obtain the best expertise possible about the future outlook for your desired occupations, companies, and industries.
Build financial independence	Moses summarizes this point very well: "To manage your career effectively, you must also manage your personal finances. When your finances are in good shape, you can make career decisions based on what is really important to you."[5] I would further add that you avoid debt at all costs (other than for home and car purchases). Live within your means and try to save at least 10% of your income and you will have greater career flexibility and freedom.

---

[3] Ibid., p. 180.

[4] Ibid., p. 185.

[5] Ibid., p. 190.

Think lattice, not ladders

The old model of climbing the corporate ladder one rung at a time has been obliterated. The new metaphor is a lattice, or as one of my former deans, Dennis Guseman, has recently written, the activity of rock climbing. You can no longer go straight up. Often you will need to move sideways and occasionally even back down the rock to find a more effective path to your desired destination.

Choose: Specialist or generalist?

Moses asserts that you should "[c]hoose a path that plays both to your strengths and the business environment. But don't carve your path in stone. Career trends are fickle, and the desirability of specialists or generalists is subject to fashion."[6] I would add that your choice depends on your profession and your career stage. In my experience, employees normally start as generalists, then they develop specialized expertise due to the nature of their roles and projects, then they have to move back to a more generalist role if they enter management positions.

Manage time ruthlessly

Due to the increasingly fast pace of work, time has become an even more scarce resource. We constantly need to remind ourselves about our priorities, and we must learn to say *no* to some activities. It is also vital to refresh and renew ourselves on a regular basis.

Don't lose yourself

Too often we beat ourselves up in the pursuit of perfection, or we get carried along in a stream of the urgent matters of others, neglecting important personal matters. Make time for personal development and never, never lose sight of what is most important to you.

 TREK TASK 31

MOSES' 12 CAREER COMMANDMENTS

Go back and review these 12 commandments carefully. Identify three specific action items that you can start doing *right now* to help your career become more successful.

---

[6] Ibid., p. 194.

SMART GOALS

Achieving career success is facilitated by setting effective career goals for yourself. Companies will often ask you where you see yourself in three years, so map out your targeted destination and establish short-term goals that will take you there. I recommend that my students create a professional mission statement that articulates their desired destinations in three years. Don't put some fuzzy, ambiguous statement about your desire for peace of mind and that you find a job where you can enjoy going to work each day. Think in terms of specific careers (occupations, companies, and/or industries). Writing such a mission statement does not mean your path is set in stone, but it will give you some focus as you develop some intermediate goals.

A commonly used acronym to describe characteristics of effective goals is SMART. SMART goals have the following characteristics:

- *Specific.* The goal should be narrowly defined to a particular accomplishment or target; don't make general goals such as "be the best employee I can be."

- *Measurable.* The goal should be measurable so that you can gauge your progress; some goals are easier to measure than others (e.g., sales targets, product defects, weight loss, etc.).

- *Actionable.* If you cannot control most of the factors that influence goal accomplishment, then set a different goal; action-oriented goals mean that you can take action that will affect the results.

- *Realistic.* Your specific, measurable goal should be realistic, something that you can attain with reasonable effort; for example, losing 10 pounds in two months is a realistic goal for me, while losing 50 pounds in two months would be unrealistic.

- *Time-based.* Give your goals a defined time frame; "I want to increase my sales revenue by 20 percent over the next three months."

 TREK TASK 32
THREE-YEAR CAREER ACTION PLAN

Complete a 3-year career action plan. Prepare a clear and concise professional mission statement (Where do you see yourself professionally in 3 years?). Identify critical milestones that will mark your progress toward that destination. Establish at least two short-term SMART goals for each of the following time periods—the next 6 months, 6 to 12 months, and 1 to 2 years.

TWO TESTS

Tom Peters provided the impetus for our Brand You concept described in Chapter 2. Let's turn to him again to describe two tests that you should take periodically to assess how well you are developing your brand. I believe they are especially

---

EXHIBIT 13.1
McKinsey Résumé Test (McKRT)

I advocated previously that you should periodically update your résumé, at least on an annual basis. Here are six specific items that Tom Peters recommends you consider when updating your résumé:

You can point to two or three completed projects.

You can enumerate, qualitatively and possibly quantitatively, the benefits delivered to your clients in each of those projects.

You can provide references—names, addresses, e-mail addresses, phone numbers, fax numbers—of living human beings, called clients, who will testify to the fact that you were alive, and doing good work, during the past year.

You can explain (precisely) what you have learned that's new and how it makes you more valuable on the labor market for your skill set.

You can point to a measurably fatter paper/electronic Rolodex, in which the preponderance of new entries will come from outside your organization rather than inside.

Should you so wish, for whatever reason, at year's end you can work up a résumé that is noticeably/discernibly/distinctly different than your résumé would have been on December 31 of the previous year.

---

important early in your career when your brand is still largely in embryonic status. They are known as the McKinsey Résumé Test[7] (McKRT—sounds like a new type of McDonald's sandwich) and the Personal Brand Equity Test (PBET).[8] See Exhibits 13.1 and 13.2.

Your résumé should be a living, dynamic document. These six items in the McKRT should help you assess the improvements to your career over a year. If you find yourself in a position where you are not working on meaningful projects (with some measurable outcomes), then it is up to you to seek them out. Help your organization solve problems, or volunteer in other organizations where you can accomplish something significant. Your résumé should become stronger each year.

Personal Brand Equity Test (PBET)

You should complete the PBET on a quarterly basis (i.e., once every 90 days or so). The items are listed in Exhibit 13.2.

---

[7] Peters, T. (1999). *Circle of innovation.* New York: Vintage, pp. 186–187.
[8] Ibid., p. 193.

EXHIBIT 13.2
PERSONAL BRAND EQUITY TEST (PBET)

I am *known for* (2–4 items); by next year at this time, I plan to also be known for (1–2 items).

My *current project* is challenging to me in (1–3 ways).

New learnings in the last 90 days include (1–3 items).

My public *visibility program* consists of (2–4 items).

Important new additions to my *network* in the last 90 days are (2–5 names).

Important *relationships* nurtured in the last 90 days include (1–3 names).

My principal *"résumé enhancement activity"* for the next 60–90 days is (1 item).

My résumé is specifically different from last year's at this time in the following (1–3 ways).

Brand equity means what it implies—the amount you have invested in the development of your unique brand. The PBET consists of eight question that help you measure how well you have been enhancing Brand You. Notice that questions 1 and 8 in Exhibit 13.1 focus on one-year time frames (one year ahead in question 1 and one year behind in question 8). Questions 2 to 7 emphasize short-term measures of your brand equity, indicators that probe continual learning, professional relationship development, and significant accomplishments. Question 4 mentions a visibility program and deserves further clarification. The point of this indicator is that you may have terrific skills and a great attitude, you may have tremendous expertise or creativity, but if your accomplishments and attributes are not visible to your organization then your brand equity is significantly reduced. This does not mean that you need to go on the campaign trail for yourself like one of the presidential candidates. All it means is that you need to pay attention to how your brand is being marketed. And ideally, your bosses, coworkers, and customers should be your best salespersons for your brand. There are many ways to improve your visibility in an organization: take on challenging, high-profile projects; go the extra mile for someone; exceed your boss's expectations; solve a tough organizational problem creatively; bring the important contributions of a coworker to the organization's attention; provide selfless community service; and always be a positive force on project teams. The bottom line is that you need to increase brand awareness without coming across as self-serving or egocentric. You can do this if you focus on being generous with your talents and time and really trying to help other people shine—you will be the one who glows!

In summary, start strong by exceeding your new company's performance expectations. Seek understanding about how you can get involved with tasks and

TREK TASK 33

PERSONAL BRAND EQUITY TEST (PBET)

Complete the PBET as an essential component in your career planning process. Ponder the eight items carefully and write down your responses to each item. Pay particular attention to questions 4 and 7.

projects that are aligned with your passion and best skills. Apply the rules of career success. And then check your short-term and annual progress by completing the two tests. Keep climbing!

Pat yourself on the back. You are doing more to effectively manage your career than most of your peers just by virtue of applying these concepts and spending more of your mental energy thinking about your career direction. But before your head gets too big, read the next chapter. All travelers attempting to reach the summit of Mount Career face challenging decisions along the way. They also have to manage the competing demands of their professional and personal domains.

TREK LIST

☐ **START STRONG**   I know what my boss expects of me; my work priorities are clearly defined.

☐ **THREE-YEAR CAREER TARGET**   I have a well-defined goal for where I want to be professionally in 3 years.

☐ **RULES FOR CAREER SUCCESS**   With my 3-year goal in mind, I identified three to five of Moses' career commandments that I want to follow which will have the biggest impact on achieving my goal.

☐ **SMART GOALS**   I know the SMART framework and have established short-term SMART goals to assist my progress toward the 3-year goal.

☐ **BRAND DEVELOPMENT**   I took the two tests by Tom Peters (McKRT and PBET) and have figured out a process to retake these tests periodically in the future.

Career Decisions

DILBERT: © Scott Adams/Dist. by United Feature Syndicate, Inc.

Recently I made a very tough career decision, the decision to leave Cal State San Marcos after six enjoyable and productive years to accept a one-year visiting position at my bachelor's degree alma mater, Brigham Young University. This personal decision offers specific insights that may be valuable to you as you are faced with challenging career decisions as you continue your ascent to the summit of your career. In this chapter three types of tough career decisions are discussed:

- Career or job change decisions
- Work–life balance decisions
- Nonmonetary versus monetary decisions

Before leaping into these decision types, I want to summarize for you four major decision-making approaches identified by scholarly research of individual decision-making activities. The four approaches are

1. Rational-economic (or optimization)
2. Administrative (or satisficing)
3. Implicit favorite
4. Intuitive

The *rational-economic* approach to making decisions was developed by economists, and therefore, it is based upon economics principles. Such principles include the assumptions that the decision maker has access to complete data about all possible alternatives, the decision maker will behave rationally, and that all possible alternatives will be evaluated so that *the best* (or optimal) decision will be made. This model worked great for economists and decisions related to markets, industries, and firms. But it doesn't work well for individual decisions, and especially not for career decisions.

The practical limitations of the rational-economic approach led researchers to closely examine how business administrators (executives and managers) actually made decisions. What they found was vastly different than the economics version of making decisions, and is known as the *administrative* approach. People do not have perfect information about all possible alternatives, nor do they have the time or the resolve in most cases to painstakingly research every possible option. So they create a small set of key criteria that can be considered their minimum standard requirements for any selected alternative. Next, instead of simultaneously evaluating all possible alternatives (as suggested by the rational-economic approach), the decision maker starts with the first identified alternative and tests it against the key criteria. If the alternative meets those criteria, it is selected. If not, the next option is considered. At the end of the day, the decision maker has made a choice that is deemed as "good enough," but not necessarily the optimal decision. Graduating students use this approach on a consistent basis. For example, often the only key criteria that a graduate identifies is a significant increase in salary from the person's current employment. The student jumps on the first job offer that comes along meeting his or her income expectations. This can be a big mistake.

The third main decision approach is called the *implicit favorite* approach, and it is a variation on the administrative approach. Because the administrative approach involves a sequential assessment of various options, a key question is "What determines which of several alternatives is evaluated first?" Well, research shows that decision makers frequently have a predetermined course of action already in their minds. In other words, for whatever reasons, an individual already has an implicitly favorite alternative that he or she wants to choose. Usually this option is evaluated first. Decision makers will usually examine a few other alternatives, if for no other reason than to give the perception to others that a thorough and objective decision has been made. In reality, the chosen option is what the decision maker preferred from the outset.

Finally, a fourth approach is known as the *intuitive* approach. That's right, the phenomenal or dreaded (depending on your perspective) female intuition. This is a decision approach made without significant analysis of data, but with a keen sense of the feelings in your gut. It typically involves mental patterns that may be hard to describe or quantify but some internal compass tends to tell you whether or not a particular decision should be made. Successful business executives believe that experience strengthens the likelihood of making effective decisions using the intuitive approach. But even experienced executives indicate that decisions made by gut instinct are sometimes wrong.

Is there a best approach for making tough career decisions? Not in my opinion, but I tend to see the last two approaches—implicit favorite and intuitive—used more for career-related decisions. However, all four approaches have some valuable elements that will be highlighted as we discuss different types of career decisions.

CAREER/JOB CHANGE DECISIONS

Individuals can decide to change for many reasons that I place in three broad categories:

- Involuntary (being fired, victim of corporate layoffs, spouse relocation)
- Voluntary—bad situation (leaving a bad manager, a bad industry or company outlook, a bad position that is deteriorating your marketability, or simply a bad fit)
- Voluntary—better opportunity (moving to a better company or industry, to a better position with greater advancement opportunities, to a better fit overall)

The involuntary changes don't require making tough decisions, except that such changes can at times free an individual to rethink his career path and consider a better fit elsewhere. The other decision for these individuals is to remain positive and not to become discouraged. Using our mountain metaphor, an involuntary exit from a company can feel like an avalanche wiping you out down the side of the mountain. Layoffs are somewhat different from terminations (the corporate term for "you're fired!"). Most companies will offer employees some form of severance package and provide some outplacement assistance to help employees find new jobs elsewhere.

The tougher decisions involve voluntary departures from organizations. How do you know when it is time to leave? You can either leave due to a perceived undesirable current situation, or you can leave when you identify a better opportunity elsewhere. Based on data from an extensive Gallup Organization study, Marcus Buckingham and Curt Coffman reach the conclusion that employees most often leave organizations because of bad managers.[1] If you have a bad manager, the question to ask is whether or not this is indicative of the type of managers throughout the organization. If so, get out. If not, you can seek a transfer within your organization, but this is not always an easy process depending on the organization's structure and the power level of your manager.

You might also consider leaving a bad situation if you believe that the company or its industry are in decline. If the company is shrinking, or if the industry has drastically changed and shifted the balance of power away from your current company, you may want to leave. Another warning sign that you may want to leave is when an organization is eroding your marketability because of its unwillingness to provide time and resources for skill development and new opportunities. If you keep doing the same thing month after month, or have hit a plateau

---

[1] Buckingham, M., & Coffman, C. (1999). *First, break all the rules: What the world's greatest managers do differently.* New York: Pocket Books.

where you have no further chance for advancement, then you should seriously consider other organizations. Finally, keep in mind the Person–Job Fit Model from Chapter 1. If the fit decreases significantly based upon permanent organizational changes, revise that resume and get ready to look elsewhere.

My decision to leave CSUSM and take a visiting position at Brigham Young University is an example of the final category of job changes—leaving for a better opportunity. In my case, I didn't have bad managers. My dean and department chair at CSUSM were great and I have deep respect for each of them. The CSU outlook, effects on my marketability, and the overall fit are definitely concerns where I thought BYU provided a better opportunity. Some of the factors I evaluated included future availability of resources, opportunities to balance teaching and research efforts, and professional and personal fit. Be careful with decisions based on the perception of a better opportunity. There is a "grass is always greener on the other side of the hill" phenomenon that can cause individuals to have unrealistic expectations of new positions. Once they change positions they find that the new position isn't perfect either. The keys are do your homework, consult your career advisors (close network members), and then trust your gut.

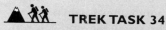

TREK TASK 34

EVALUATING PERSON–JOB FIT: THE SEQUEL

Evaluate the fit of your current position (consider the nature of the position, the company, and the industry). Try to project where the company and industry will be in 3 years and what role you would be playing at that time. Any warning signs indicating this is a bad situation?

WORK–LIFE BALANCE DECISIONS

Kristin Farmer, CEO of Autistic Comprehensive Educational Services (ACES), made an unusual comment to me. She said, "Becoming more balanced in my life has actually helped me make better business decisions." I personally believe that balance is important to your success professionally and in life. In life, I subscribe to Stephen Covey's description of the benefits of balancing the spiritual, physical, social, and mental dimensions of your life.[2] However, one of the toughest challenges in the current environment is to effectively balance the intense demands from both work and nonwork domains. With professionals working an average of 50 to 55 hours per week, and with customers expecting 24/7 service, obtaining any type of balance is a daunting task.

Many of my students have asked me how I maintain balance given my wife and five children. They have also asked how you can know when the imbalance becomes

---

[2] Covey, S. (1996). *First things first.* Wichita, KS: Fireside Publishing.

excessive. I have a fundamental assumption about careers that you may or may not agree with, but you need to understand it to make sense of these thoughts about balance. *Your career should be the means to achieve other ends; it should not be an end in and of itself.* My profession sends signals to others about what I do, but it does not define who I am. With that assumption, here are some steps to consider:

1. You need to be honest and examine the relative salience of each of the two domains (work and nonwork). Not all persons desire work–life balance. Some individuals are workaholics and that domain is far more essential to them than the nonwork domain. For me, my family will always take priority over my career. The key is self-awareness. *How much balance do you truly want?*

2. Kristin Farmer mentioned that finding the right partner—her husband—has made the achievement of balance so much easier. From my own experience, I submit that the decision you make about who you spend your life with is your most important decision in life. As Chapter 6 emphasized, surrounding yourself with great people is vital to success on this career journey. It is no less important to surround yourself with the right people in your nonwork domain (i.e., spouse, partner, children, close friends). Many a career has been derailed because the person has made poor choices about a spouse or friends. I cannot overstate how supportive my sweet wife and companion, Jennifer, has been in my career. Any successes I have achieved have been her successes as well. She is my best friend. We trust each other without question. She knows at the end of the day that her happiness is my number-one priority. Perhaps you've heard the saying, "Behind any successful man is a great woman—and a surprised mother-in-law." Well, my wife did not marry me for any wealth or fame that I possessed. Instead, she married largely on faith in my potential. Her belief in my capabilities and complementary talents in some of my weaker areas have made all the difference in my career. *Choose a talented, supportive companion.*

3. When you enter a committed relationship with someone else (spouse or significant other) you need to *clearly communicate your career expectations with each other.* When my wife and I decided to get married, we discussed our aspirations about our careers and how we would work together to provide financial means for our future family. We decided from the outset that while we had young children in our home, my wife would be a "stay-at-home" mother to provide that type of environment for our children. This does not need to be the expectation you have about your career. My point is that you need to have this conversation with each other early in a serious relationship. You need to clarify expectations at work to be successful. You also need to confirm expectations about work with those closest to you if you want to achieve any type of balance.

4. *You need to know and manage expectations of your work relationships.* My colleagues know that my family is important to me and that I am not likely to frequently go golfing or to Friday happy hours with them. It is also more difficult for me to attend evening and weekend events. Some

executives set clear boundaries about time spent with family and time spent on work-related activities. They will keep Sundays free from work and focus on those days as family days. Or they will leave work by 6:00 p.m. to ensure being at home for dinner on weeknights. This does not mean that they won't do some work at home late in the evening, but they make time for those important to them.

5. *Refresh yourself regularly.* Among my most cherished childhood memories are the family vacations when my father got away from work for a few days and we could spend time together. Whether you have a family or not, I believe it is absolutely essential to your career and personal well-being to get away from work responsibilities from time to time. Europeans have made time off from work into an art form. Most U.S. companies offer two weeks paid vacation, and it still amazes me how many employees do not take advantage of all of those 10 business days off. Some companies have even adopted the academic model of paid sabbaticals for their employees. Burnout is a common professional hazard in our country. Avoid it by spending time with personal hobbies and passions outside of work. Physical muscles need rest and time to rejuvenate. Your professional muscles need the same opportunities for recuperation.

6. *Include your spouse (or significant other) in every major career decision.* Never, ever make a major career move without consulting with your spouse. This is a no-brainer if you really love your spouse, plus that person should know you better than anyone else and can give you sound advice on the potential fit of diverse opportunities. I have encountered numerous company CEOs who use and trust their spouses as sounding boards for important business decisions. Your spouse should definitely be a member of your career board of directors.

7. *Seek companies that value employee work–life balance.* If you desire greater balance, find out *before you accept an offer* what the company's attitudes are toward work–life balance. You can assess this by learning of the company's work–life programs and policies, by asking questions of your interviewers, and talking with company employees who have similar family structures as you.

8. *Recognize the trade-offs.* Achieving work–life balance does require trade-offs. Our decision to have five children and for my wife to stay home with our children has meant that we are a single-income family with minimal discretionary income. In Southern California, that was not easy. It means I drive a 1990 Geo Prizm, not a Lexus or a BMW. It means that I will not be as prolific in publishing research as some of my colleagues because I just do not have the time to do so. However, it also means that I remain less obsessed with my work activities. When I walk through my front door in the evening after a day at work, one of my younger children comes running and smiling, so happy that I am home. My children don't care if my research submission has been rejected by another journal, or if I sat through (seemingly) endless committee meetings that day. They just want to play and want a few minutes of my time and attention.

Can you have a great family and a great career? You absolutely can! But it takes considerable attention, effort, and teamwork from both family members and coworkers to accomplish that mission. It also can mean that you have to adjust your definition of "great" somewhat if you are trying to have it all. I have told my students many times that balance was the primary factor in my decision to shift careers from a technology and business consultant to a business professor. Would I be making more money now if I had remained with Andersen Consulting? Yes, considerably more. Would I have spent as much time with my wife and my children if I had stayed with Andersen Consulting? No, considerably less. That is a trade that I will take anytime!

NONMONETARY VERSUS MONETARY DECISIONS

One of the most common decisions that you will have to make along the way is the decision of whether to follow your passion or the money. It is common for individuals to say, "I love what I do but it just doesn't pay very well." It is very enticing, especially when you have been living on a student budget, to jump at the opportunity to make more money. And if that opportunity allows you to do what you do best more frequently then I say all the more power to you. However, be careful about leaving your passion to pursue more income.

The overwhelming majority of successful executives with whom I have interacted live by this rule: "Follow your passion and the money will follow." I believe that, but it is not quite as simple as they make it sound. You have to be somewhat realistic about market demands for your passions. I am very passionate about teaching and I love what I do, but I don't expect to make millions of dollars annually as a business professor. On the other hand, there are many rich people in this nation who do *not* have much passion for what they do—they are just very good (or very lucky) at what they do. What you need to keep in mind is that there is more to any business decision than just the monetary elements. Remember this:

Passion + Practice → Performance → Payoffs

The size of those payoffs are dependent upon the value that customers place on those performances. Make sure that your career decisions allow you to be in a position to perform at your highest level and where customers—internal or external—perceive the value of your performance distinctly from other performers.

TREK LIST

☐ **JOB/CAREER CHANGE DECISIONS**   I understand the major reasons for job or career changes and have reflected on whether or not a change would be best for me.

☐ **WORK–LIFE BALANCE DECISIONS**   I have talked with my spouse/partner (if applicable) about work priorities and life priorities; I make time each week for some form of personal development.

☐ **PASSION OR MONEY**   Try to achieve both—but I will always err on the side of passion.

Mentoring and Professional Development

[A]s the executive champion of our corporate mentoring program, I try to listen to my mentees and determine the next opportunity for their developmental experience. It's also helpful to chat with folks about what I am dealing with on a daily basis; it gives them an opportunity to see things in a more holistic way. What's more, mentoring helps me stay grounded in employees' realities.

A mentor has to make sure that the conversation around continuous development is inspiring, not intimidating. A great leader truly believes that personal development is a never-ending journey. If you can help people embrace and love continuous development, then you are really making a difference in their lives and careers.

—*Betsy Bernard (former President, AT&T)* [1]

Obtaining your first professional position is exhilarating, but it does not represent the summit of your career. You can do all the right things in your first year of employment, but there is still much more climbing to be done. How do individuals reach the top of Everest? According to Krakauer's account, very few reach the summit without experienced guides. It is also beneficial to have honed one's mountaineering skills by climbing summits of lesser stature and difficulty first. I liken these two factors of mountain-climbing success to the career tools of mentoring and professional development activities. In this concluding chapter of *Career Trek,* we explore these two activities that will increase your chances of a successful career.

MENTORING

Having completed a doctoral dissertation on the subject and having conducted several research projects on both mentoring relationships and mentoring programs, it is clear that mentoring relationships have several advantages for career success.

---

[1] Haley, F., & Canabou, C. (2003, October). Fast talk: The mentors' mentors. *Fast Company,* vol. 75, p. 59.

However, there are some potential costs and obstacles that you need to understand. At the end of this section on mentoring, you should have learned the following:

- Mentoring defined (including distinctions between formal and informal mentoring)
- Potential benefits and costs of mentoring (to both individuals and to the organization)
- A prescribed network of mentors that will accelerate your career advancement

Mentoring Defined

Mentoring can be defined as a unique interpersonal relationship between a more experienced individual (the mentor) and a less experienced individual (the protégé), wherein the mentor functions as a role model for the protégé and provides support and encouragement for the protégé's career and personal development. Inherent in this definition are the three main functions that mentors provide to protégés:

1. Career development activities—personal coaching, skills training, challenging assignments
2. Social support activities—counseling, friendship and encouragement, confidence building
3. Role modeling activities—professional conduct, behavioral knowledge, detailed feedback

Over the past 20 years, mentoring has received greater attention in organizations as a means of developing organizational members in a cost-effective manner. In companies such as Intel and Edward Jones, mentoring is a formalized activity used to train specific skills in newer employees. Formal mentoring programs started to appear in companies in the late 1980s and have become more commonplace in the current business environment. Whereas informal mentoring relationships develop naturally between organizational members, formal mentoring relationships are mandated by an organizational program. Depending on the parameters of the mentoring program, participants may have some choice in who their mentoring partner will be. However, it is still an assigned relationship. Research on formal mentoring programs has shown that they can vary greatly in terms of their effectiveness.

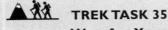 **TREK TASK 35**

WHO ARE YOUR MENTORS?

Given the mentoring definition previously given, identify any individuals you currently view as your mentors. If you cannot identify a mentor, think about one person in your work or academic organization you believe would be a good mentor to you, given your career aspirations.

Mentoring Benefits and Costs

Protégé Benefits. Why should you strive to have a mentor? Research over the past 15 years has demonstrated significant positive relationships between having a mentor and the following important outcomes:[2]

- Rate of promotion
- Salary growth
- Amount of personal learning
- Job satisfaction
- Employee commitment
- Intentions to stay with an organization (i.e., lower turnover rates)
- Balancing work and family demands
- Perceived career success

Protégés benefit from mentoring relationships in many ways. Mentors help protégés develop skills necessary for future promotions. Not only will they guide protégés in identifying the needed skills, but they also provide opportunities and feedback for their protégés to actually develop those skills. Mentors assist protégés by giving them access to the mentors' professional networks, which are typically larger and more influential. By placing protégés in high-profile assignments and introducing them to key organizational decision makers, mentors often increase the visibility of their protégés, which tends to result in better opportunities for advancement.

Protégé Costs. The biggest cost for both the protégé and the mentor is the time investment to manage the relationship effectively. As with other interpersonal relationships, mentoring takes commitment in time and energy, especially on the front end of the relationship, to develop trust, to define expectations, to establish goals, and to understand one another's skills and personalities. Beyond the time commitment are other potential costs to consider. Most of them are less likely to occur if you have an effective, trusted mentor. Because mentors rely primarily on their own experiences and knowledge base, protégés need to be careful that the information and advice they receive is still relevant given industry or societal trends. In other words, are the mentors offering outdated information? Another issue is that occasional mentors may exploit their protégés to avoid performing work activities they find unpleasant. Good mentors will focus instead on the work activities protégés should be performing successfully to advance their careers. Two potential protégé costs that exist when working with effective mentors are (a) overdependence on the mentor; and (b) resentment by the protégé's peers. There comes a time in all mentoring relationships where the protégé needs to separate and become independent from the mentor's watchful

---

[2] For a thorough review of mentoring benefits and overall literature review of mentoring activities, please see Higgins & Kram (2001, *Academy of Management Review*), Lankau, Carlson, & Nielson (2006, *Journal of Vocational Behavior*), Lankau & Scandura (2002, *Academy of Management Journal*), or Ragins, Cotton, & Miller (2000, *Journal of Applied Psychology*).

guidance. This could happen if the protégé takes a job at another organization or is promoted elsewhere within the same organization. In cases where the protégé came to see the mentor as a true role model and came to rely on the mentor heavily for career guidance, this separation can be problematic. Such protégés can struggle at times to make decisions independently and miss the frequent feedback that was typically provided by their mentors. The protégé's peers may also resent the mentoring relationship, particularly if they think that similar opportunities to obtain mentoring assistance were not available to them. Research indicates that peer perceptions are a particularly challenging issue for cross-gender mentoring relationships (i.e., male mentor–female protégé, female mentor–male protégé).

Reputation, Reputation, Reputation. The reputation of both parties can be a double-edged sword. In organizations where the mentoring pairings are well known, through either formal or informal communication channels, there is a "reputation by association" phenomenon. If the mentor's power and influence in the organization rises, so will that of the mentor's protégés. Conversely, if the mentor's stock falls, so will that of the protégés to some extent. A similar issue exists from the mentor's perspective. If a protégé's stock rises in an organization while under the mentor's tutelage, then the mentor will acquire a reputation as a valuable developer of the organization's talent. However, if the protégé was viewed by organizational leaders as a rising star and then falls short of those expectations during the mentoring relationship, then the protégé's career advancement will take a hit, and so will the reputation of the mentor.

Mentor Benefits. From my own research and that of other mentoring scholars, the most common benefit cited by mentors is simply the personal fulfillment they receive when sharing their accumulated wisdom with others and knowing that they helped other people become more successful in their careers and/or in life. Mentors often describe being on the receiving end of mentoring help earlier in their careers, and providing mentoring help to newer employees fulfills a need to give back. This benefit may be particularly important to mentors above the age of 50, who may feel that their organizations are slowly pushing them toward retirement with less challenging assignments. Other benefits mentioned by mentors include job rejuvenation, establishment of a group of loyal supporters in the organization, enhancing creativity, and the aforementioned reputation as a developer of talent. The creativity benefit deserves special emphasis as organizations strive for innovation to gain or maintain competitive advantages. How do mentoring activities stimulate creative ideas? It is the mixture of old and new thinking. Mentors know how their organizations and industries work. Protégés, however, may come up with new ideas from other employers or from their formal educations programs. This is especially true related to knowledge of new technologies. An example of this benefit occurred at General Electric as reported in the *Wall Street Journal*. Leading GE executives were paired with younger employees who were more savvy about the Internet. They combined the Internet knowledge with the business and industry expertise of the executives to come up with ideas for how GE could best leverage the Internet in the company.

Mentor Costs. When asked why they would not participate in mentoring activities, the two most common responses given by managers are the time commitment involved to do it right (discussed previously), and the perception that it was an activity that went unrewarded at most organizations. Personal experience suggests that the second cost is generally true. Most organizations do not formally or directly reward their employees for being strong mentors. It can be argued that mentoring should not be monetarily rewarded, at least not immediately. Otherwise, mentors may do it more for the money than to actually help the protégé. One other potential cost is the threat of opportunistic protégés making the mentor's job in an organization less tenable. For example, a mentor trains a protégé how to perform the essential elements of the mentor's job. The mentor does this under the assumption that she will be promoted soon and then the protégé can be promoted to the mentor's position. In some cases, organizations have instead reasoned that they can fire the mentor (removing her higher salary) and promote the protégé (at a lower salary than the mentor) because the protégé has learned how to perform the mentor's job. If there is precedent for this type of behavior at your company—watch your back!

Organization Benefits. Many companies in the past 10 years, having observed the benefits to employees of informal mentoring activities, have attempted to formalize the mentoring process by creating mentoring programs. Mentoring strengthens organizations in at least four ways. First, mentoring provides organizations with a cost-effective method for improving the skill development of less-experienced employees. Not only is this method of training cost-effective, but because mentoring tends to be a one-to-one relationship, the training is tailored to the talents and needs of the protégé. Second, mentoring perpetuates the core values of the organization along with essential knowledge and routines. One of the common activities provided by the mentor is to reinforce an organization's cultural values, both through the mentor's example and through the telling of organizational stories that highlight those values. Third, organizations have found that having a reputation for being a mentoring organization is attractive to talented prospective employees and can help organizations retain those employees. Savvy job seekers know that increasing their marketability is one key to their career success. If mentoring is available, encouraged, and effective, they can count that as both a short-term and a long-term benefit. Mentors may also wield some influence in helping protégés make major career decisions. In some cases, protégés will even feel a sense of obligation to stay with their current organizations primarily because of their mentors' investments in their careers. Finally, organizations often create mentoring programs to target high-potential employees and/or minority employees to help them develop their leadership potential and become the next wave of leaders.

Organization Costs. Mentors tend to perpetuate organizational values and routines that have worked in the past and made themselves and their organizations successful. What happens if the organizational environment dramatically changes? Will those past routines and values predict future success? This is a constant concern in our rapidly changing world, but mentoring speeds the perpetuation process and may result in protégés that leave past assumptions unquestioned. Another danger to the organization is that the implementation of formal mentoring programs may result in perceptions of inequity based upon which employees are allowed to participate and how those decisions are made. For example, suppose that your company has a mentoring program for what it calls "high-potential" employees. Suppose further that you are not selected for that program but some of your peers are selected. How will that affect your commitment toward the organization? How will it affect your perceptions of those peers in the program? Organizations must be extremely cautious that mentoring programs do not become divisive elements in the company culture. The final potential cost to organizations is that they may lose talented employees as those employees develop more marketable skills from the mentoring activities. This can frequently be the case if there are few opportunities for advancement in the protégé's current organization. In the late 1990s, why were so many Microsoft executives lured away to dot-com startups? In part, it was because they had worked with Bill Gates and Steve Ballmer, and the dot-coms hoped that they would bring their learning gained from mentoring with those two highly respected individuals.

Table 15.1 summarizes the benefits and costs of mentoring for protégés, mentors, and organizations. It may be apparent already, but I clearly view mentoring as a valuable activity in which the benefits almost always outweigh the costs. Now for something really radical: I will suggest that you develop a network of mentors to help you guide your career.

TABLE 15.1   SUMMARY OF MENTORING BENEFITS AND COSTS

	Benefits	Costs
Protégé	Faster promotions/opportunities for advancement Salary growth Learning and skill development Job satisfaction Employee commitment Perceived career success Reputation as mentor's stock rises	Time and energy commitment Outdated information Overdependence on mentor Mentor exploitation Resentment by peers Reputation as mentor's stock falls
Mentor	Personal fulfillment Job rejuvenation Cadre of loyal supporters Creative new ideas Reputation as developer of talent	Time and energy commitment Activity not rewarded by organization Threat of opportunistic protégés Reputation as destroyer of talent
Organization	Cost-effective training method Culture and key routines perpetuated Tool for talent attraction and retention Leadership development	Equity concerns Perpetuates outdated knowledge May lose more marketable employees to competitors

Mentoring Network

Back in Chapter 2, I introduced the concept of you as the CEO of your own career. Now I recommend to you that you establish a network of trusted mentors who will act as a career advisory board to you. Let me explain why I advocate this approach. Given the benefits that have been reported from having a mentor, I encourage you to forge mentoring relationships. However, if you have but a single mentor it is somewhat analogous to investing all of your money in only one stock. If that mentor leaves your organization, is the victim of a company downsizing, or because of other events declines in power and influence, you suffer as well. It is not advisable in today's business environment to put all of your mentoring eggs into a single basket. A second reason for establishing a network of mentors is to enable you to draw from the diverse skills and knowledge of multiple professionals. It is increasingly unlikely that you will find a single mentor who possesses all of the skills and knowledge you desire to be successful in your career. So seek out multiple mentors.

What type of network makes the most sense? A network of three to five mentors makes the most sense given the time commitment needed to develop such relationships. If your immediate supervisor is open to it, he or she should be considered as a possible mentor. I also suggest someone higher up in the organizational hierarchy but not your boss's boss. You may also identify a third individual in the organization who may have a specific skill set you need to acquire. Finally, I recommend that you have at least one (and perhaps more than one) mentor whose knowledge and experience you respect but who does not work in your organization.

 TREK TASK 36

DEVELOPING A MENTORING NETWORK

Use the guidelines in the previous paragraph to establish your mentoring network. Are there any holes in your network? Any skills/knowledge areas that are not being met by your current mentors? Start identifying individuals you trust who could provide the type of mentoring assistance you need to advance in your career.

PROFESSIONAL DEVELOPMENT

Mentoring, while an important method of professional development, describes only part of the process. In an important study published in 2001, authors from McKinsey Consulting reported that developing employees was one of five essential steps to win what the authors called "the war for talent."[3] They described a concept called the Employee Value Proposition, which helps organizations answer the question, "Why would people want to come work in our organization?" Growth and development opportunities was one of four key aspects they

---

[3] Michaels, H-J., & Axelrod. (2001). *The war for talent.* Boston: Harvard Business School Publishing.

identified from their research that prospective employees look at when considering an employer. You should be paying attention to it, too.

In addition to looking for mentoring opportunities, you should consider four other development avenues. They are

1. *Stretch goals/high-profile projects.* If you find that your current work is not sufficiently challenging or that your skills are stagnating, seek out stretch opportunities. This can be done with work-related or school-related projects. Find out which projects are highest in priority and volunteer to become involved on those projects. Employers love employees who demonstrate initiative and a willingness to take some risks in order to accomplish important projects and to develop new skills.

2. *Performance feedback.* In your first year with a company, or even during the latter stages of the interview process, you should become familiar with the company's performance review process. If the company is consistent with the majority of organizations, there may be only an annual review of your performance. That is not enough to effectively develop your skills and professional expertise. Try to establish an open relationship with whomever you report to so that you can seek performance feedback on an ongoing basis. Consistent with this avenue of development, you have to learn to take constructive criticism and use it to improve your performance.

3. *Formal training programs.* I was fortunate to be involved in designing the first formal training program for employees at Proflowers.com a few years ago. Our goal, given the company's resources at the time, was simply to ensure that employees attend at least 20 hours of professional development training during their fiscal year. It was a bit surprising to me how excited employees were about 20 hours of training. There is both a practical and a symbolic value in providing training opportunities to employees. Look for companies that have strong training programs. This shows that employers see employees as an investment. Once you have joined an organization make sure you clearly know what training opportunities exist and how you can take advantage of them.

4. *Job rotation programs.* The final development opportunity is to participate in a job rotation program if the organization offers one. You will need to learn the requirements for participation in the program; they are great vehicles to expose employees to diverse areas of the company's business. These programs assist employees to understand the big picture, how different departments work together, and which aspect of the business for which the employees are most suited. If your organization is too small to have a formal job rotation program, talk with your decision makers about starting a small-scale version of one. Or seek opportunities to learn about all aspects of your company's business via informal means. You won't regret the broad exposure to the organization.

TREK TASK 37

DEVELOPMENTAL OPPORTUNITIES

What is the one skill you want to improve in the next 6 months? Identify at least one developmental opportunity available to you at work or school that will help you improve your chosen skill.

With the conclusion of this chapter, we come to the end of our trek together. I hope I have given you valuable tools, tips, tasks, and strategies to help you improve your career situation now and into the future. Remember the initial lessons of fit and passion. Keep in touch with your network, but perhaps more importantly, keep in touch with yourself. One parting thought—the fruits of career success are never as sweet when you partake of them alone! I wish you well on your continued career trek up whatever mountains you decide to climb.

TREK LIST

☐ **MENTORING**   I have identified individuals who are (or could become) my mentors.

☐ **PROS AND CONS**   I recognize that as in other relationships, mentoring relationships have potential advantages and disadvantages. I am familiar with the most common of those pros and cons.

☐ **DEVELOPMENTAL PLAN**   From the mentioned developmental choices, I have identified one skill that I need to develop and I have created a plan to strengthen that area.

INDEX